ANDREW PODNIEKS

# FAST ICE
# SUPERSTARS
## *of the* NEW NHL

Published by ECW Press
665 Gerrard Street East
Toronto, Ontario, Canada M4M 1Y2
416-694-3348 | info@ecwpress.com

Editor for the press: Michael Holmes
Cover images: Dmytro Aksonov/iStockPhoto;
Jack Eichel © Kevin Hoffman/USA TODAY
Sports - RTS3NSZ; Connor McDavid © Sergei
Belski/USA TODAY Sports - RTX28WDE; P.K.
Subban © Christopher Hanewinckel/USA TODAY
Sports - RTX33OD4; Auston Matthews © John E.
Sokolowski/USA TODAY Sports - RTX2TAV5;
Sidney Crosby © Charles LeClaire/USA TODAY
Sports - RTX2EEOA

Purchase the print edition
and receive the eBook free!
For details, go to ecwpress.com/eBook.

LIBRARY AND ARCHIVES CANADA
CATALOGUING IN PUBLICATION

Podnieks, Andrew, author
Fast ice : superstars of the new NHL /
Andrew Podnieks.

Issued in print and electronic formats.
ISBN 978-1-77041-429-7 (softcover).
Also issued as: ISBN 978-1-77305-118-5 (PDF),
978-1-77305-119-2 (ePUB)

1. Hockey players—Biography.
2. National Hockey League.
I. TITLE.

GV848.5.A1P63 2017    796.962092'2
C2017-902404-3   C2017-902983-5

The publication of *Fast Ice* has been generously supported by the Government of Canada through the Canada
Book Fund. *Ce livre est financé en partie par le gouvernement du Canada.* We also acknowledge the contribution
of the Government of Ontario through the Ontario Book Publishing Tax Credit and the Ontario Media
Development Corporation.

PRINTED AND BOUND IN CANADA          PRINTING: NORECOB   5   4   3   2   1

# INTRODUCTION

The NHL of today is radically different from the game of even a decade ago. The seemingly impossible trend of making players bigger, faster, and stronger every year has continued, but scoring has also declined with relentless consistency. Wayne Gretzky's Oilers from the mid-1980s now look like a relic of some lost era of offence.

But, perhaps, even in the last few years the most dramatic change in the game has been a shift away from fighting to a reliance on speed and skill. The goon is gone. The enforcer is dead. The tough guy is a beast of the past. In his place is youth with blistering shots, incredible skating ability, and high-velocity playmaking.

And if there is one reason for this change, it cannot be found in the rule book. The NHL has done nothing to curb fighting, to outlaw the tap on the shin followed by the vehement, "Wanna go?" followed by the inevitable fight between each team's tough guy.

No. The reason can, more or less, be pinpointed to one man — current Toronto head coach Mike Babcock. Babcock has been a coach in the NHL since 2002. In his 14 years, he has won the Stanley Cup once, been in the finals two other times, and missed the playoffs only twice. He has coached exactly 150 playoff games during his league tenure, more than any other coach.

Here's what's amazing: His team has finished dead last in fighting majors in nine of his 14 seasons. He finished 29th one time and never higher than 15th, which he accomplished during the 2016–17 season with the Leafs.

Babcock has made one thing clear during his time with Anaheim (two seasons), Detroit (10 seasons), and Toronto (two seasons and counting): winning is what counts. Toughness isn't beating up an opponent; it's scoring a timely goal. Intimidation isn't a line brawl; it's playing flawless defence every third period, all season long.

You want to scare an opponent? Babcock can roll four skilled lines. That's scary. The very idea of a thug with little skill beyond boxing ability replacing a talented player in the lineup is the antithesis to the way he thinks. Fear factor? How about a centreman whose pure speed allows him to blow by those less-talented players to create scoring chances, score goals, and win games? A tough team out of the playoffs is no fan's dream.

And guess what? The rest of the league has taken notice. Fighting has dropped precipitously in the last 15 seasons. It's still a part of the game, and it's still penalized leniently, but the obvious correlation to fighting declining is that there are fewer fighters in the game.

In 2016–17, the most penalized player was Mark Borowiecki of Ottawa with 154 PIMs. Even just six years ago that total would have placed him 13th. Most of the tough guys, goons, PIMs leaders of the last several years aren't even in the NHL any more — Zenon Konopka, Daniel Carcillo, Colton Orr, Steve Downie. They are all gone. Not enough skill to keep up.

The league has very quickly made fighting an outdated style of play. Another contributing factor to the decline of fighting and the increase in skill is the ever-greater importance of the international game. First there was the Canada Cup, starting in 1976; then the greater number of European players drafted into the NHL, from the 1980s and on; then, greater NHL participation in the World Championships. In 1998, the final frontier was reached when the NHL shut down to allow its players to play at the Nagano Olympics.

In 1972, NHL players and Europeans never met. In 2017, the top stars in the NHL are also international stars, from the World Junior Championship, to the Worlds, World Cup, and Olympics. In IIHF competition, a fighting major is accompanied by a game misconduct, a one-game suspension, and an automatic review to determine if further disciplinary action is necessary.

In 1972, NHL players had never played top European players, but after the Summit Series, the comingling began. In the last quarter century, nearly 25 percent of all NHL players have come from Europe.

Different eras have produced different kinds of players and different styles of physical activity on ice. In the old days, star players learned to protect themselves, but there was mutual respect (i.e., no checking from behind, head shots, knee-on-knee checks).

In the days of the classic so-called Original Six, the top players fought their own fights (think Howe, Orr, Mikita). In the 1970s and '80s, the top players had bodyguards. The recent passing of Dave Semenko recalled the greatest of those days. Semenko patrolled the ice, fighting anyone who dared to check Wayne Gretzky. As a result, Gretzky earned more space on the ice and set records that are out of this world.

In the 1990s and early 2000s, there was the goon. He fought only the goons on other teams, played about five minutes of meaningless time per game, and served no purpose but to "entertain" the fans. But under the winning ways of Babcock, the NHL has room only for skaters, passers, shooters, scorers.

Is this another phase? Will it give way to even fewer altercations or rules that all but eliminate fighting? If opponents start to target the superstars of today — Connor McDavid, Auston Matthews, Patrik Laine — will coaches be forced to bring in tough guys again?

This might not even be possible. Junior leagues in Canada are instituting rules to curb fighting. The NCAA, which is providing more and more players for the NHL, has always banned fighting. European junior leagues have never encouraged or developed that style of play. The next generation of hockey players might well develop without ever having been involved in or seen a fight.

*Fast Ice* is a celebration of the league's transformation. It is a celebration of the game's greatest players, all of whom possess resumes loaded with achievement based on skill, not fists. The modern NHL player is young and quick with speed to burn. None of the players profiled herein has a notable fight to his credit, but they all have big goals, Stanley Cups, gold medals, and a future of greatness based on offence and agility.

**ANDREW PODNIEKS**
Toronto, August 2017

FAST
ICE

Apart from the top-player selections, the NHL Entry Draft is a lottery as much as it is an opportunity. Case in point: Cam Atkinson. Drafted in the distant sixth round in 2008, Atkinson has slowly and steadily developed into one of the top scorers in the NHL — and no one could have predicted that a decade ago.

Atkinson's ambitions were high even as a young teenager. He moved away from home at age 15 and attended Avon Old Farms, a prep high school in Connecticut that had previously developed Hall of Famer Brian Leetch and Stanley Cup–winning goaltender Jonathan Quick.

Despite averaging nearly a goal per game over three years with the Winged Beavers, Atkinson was never on the radar of USA Hockey for U18 or U20 tournaments. When he became draft eligible in 2007, exactly zero NHL teams showed interest.

The reason? Atkinson was small. Even now at 5'8" and 182 pounds, he is small to be doing such miraculous things in the NHL; as a teen, he was even less intimidating. But what he had was great skating ability and quickness. He could make plays at top speed and could simply outskate many opponents.

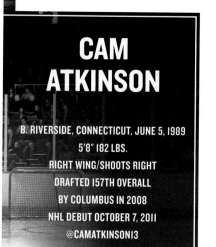

**CAM ATKINSON**

B. RIVERSIDE, CONNECTICUT, JUNE 5, 1989
5'8" 182 LBS.
RIGHT WING/SHOOTS RIGHT
DRAFTED 157TH OVERALL
BY COLUMBUS IN 2008
NHL DEBUT OCTOBER 7, 2011
@CAMATKINSON13

After being selected by the Blue Jackets in his second year of eligibility, the 19-year-old attended Boston College that fall, beginning a three-year stint there that saw him develop far beyond anyone's expectations.

In 2010–11, in what proved to be his final year of college hockey, Atkinson led the NCAA with 30 goals and took BC to the championship game where the Eagles defeated Wisconsin, 5–0. Atkinson had two goals for the winners and, soon after, was sent by the Blue Jackets to finish the season with their AHL affiliate in Springfield.

Showing no signs of being overwhelmed, he scored three times in five games. The Jackets signed him to a pro contract, and his college days were over. Atkinson was en route to the NHL.

The next year, he started the season with Columbus, making his NHL debut on October 7, 2011. He scored his first NHL goal in his third game, but after five games he was sent back to Springfield. After scoring 29 goals in 51 games — and playing in the AHL's All-Star Game — he was recalled by Columbus in late February and stayed the rest of the year. Atkinson finished strongly, recording 10 points in his final six games, including his first career hat trick.

At season's end, and the Jackets out of the playoffs, Atkinson was invited by Team USA to play at the World Championship in Sweden and Finland. He accepted and was impressive on a young and fast American team that lost a tight 3–2 game to Finland in the quarter-finals.

Atkinson seemed to get stuck in neutral the next year, splitting the season evenly between the NHL and AHL. But in 2013–14, he turned the corner. Playing the whole season with Columbus,

he scored 21 goals and proved that speed and skill — and a phenomenal shot — could trump size and strength.

Over the course of the next four seasons, Atkinson improved his goal production each year, going from 21 to 22, 27, and 35 by 2016–17. Only seven players put the puck in the net more often than Atkinson in 2016–17, with Sidney Crosby leading the league with 44.

Midway through that season, he was named to play in the NHL's All-Star Game at the Staples Center in Los Angeles as a replacement for the injured Evgeni Malkin. It was fitting: many thought Atkinson should have been named to the game initially.

In the 2017 playoffs, though, the Jackets were eliminated by Crosby and the Penguins in five games in the first round. Atkinson was limited to two goals, but the playoffs were only his second such experience.

At season's end, Atkinson tweeted, "It's been a fun year, Columbus. Thank you as always to #5thline [diehard Jackets fans] for cheering loud. See you next year."

It has been a decade since Atkinson started his ascent. From prep hockey to leading scorer in the NCAA to a top scorer in the NHL, the diminutive and skilled forward has proven skeptics wrong and rewarded Blue Jackets scouts who took a late chance on him in 2008.

Batman and Robin. Simon and Garfunkel. Butch Cassidy and the Sundance Kid.

Hockey's equivalent: Ovi and Backstrom.

Nicklas Backstrom has been serving as Alexander Ovechkin's top setup man for the last decade with the Washington Capitals, and he is also a star in his own right. Backstrom became the franchise's all-time leader in assists before reaching his 30th birthday.

The slick Swedish centre is among the best passers and two-way players in the world. His skating and shooting are also world class, but perhaps the quality of his game that is most under-appreciated is that he makes Ovechkin a better player.

A native of Gavle, Sweden, Backstrom is the son of a hockey-playing father — who spent 10 years with the local team, Brynas — and an equally athletic mother — a Finnish native who was an elite handball player.

Backstrom got his hockey start with Brynas's junior squads. He graduated to the senior men's team during the 2004–05 season but wasn't able to establish himself then at that level due to the high number of locked-out NHL players plying their trade in Europe that season.

As a result, Backstrom spent most of the 2004–05 campaign with the Brynas Under-20 team. At age 17, in April 2005, he recorded five points as Sweden won the bronze medal at the IIHF U18 World Championship.

Once the NHL got back to business in 2005–06, Backstrom quickly rose through the ranks, establishing himself as Brynas's top-line centre, and being named rookie of the year in the Swedish Elite League and top junior player in Sweden. At 18 years old, playing in his first World Junior Championship in 2006, he was Sweden's leading scorer with seven points.

## NICKLAS BACKSTROM

B. GAVLE, SWEDEN, NOVEMBER 23, 1987
6'1" 213 LBS.
CENTRE/SHOOTS LEFT
DRAFTED 4TH OVERALL
BY WASHINGTON IN 2006
NHL DEBUT OCTOBER 5, 2007
@BACKSTROM19

At age 18, the draft-eligible Backstrom became the youngest player ever to play for the Swedish national team at the 2006 men's World Championship in Latvia. A late addition, he didn't record a point in four games but did win a gold medal while skating on Sweden's top line with Henrik Zetterberg and Johan Franzen.

In June 2006, Backstrom was selected fourth overall by Washington in the NHL draft. At the time, it was the fourth-highest draft position in history for a Swedish player, behind Mats Sundin (first, 1989) and the Sedin twins (second and third, 1999).

After being drafted, Backstrom elected to continue his development in Sweden for another year. He increased his offensive output to 40 points in 45 games to lead his team in scoring in 2006–07 and was named captain of Sweden's 2007 entry at the World Junior Championship, collecting seven assists in seven games as the Swedes settled for a fourth-place finish on home

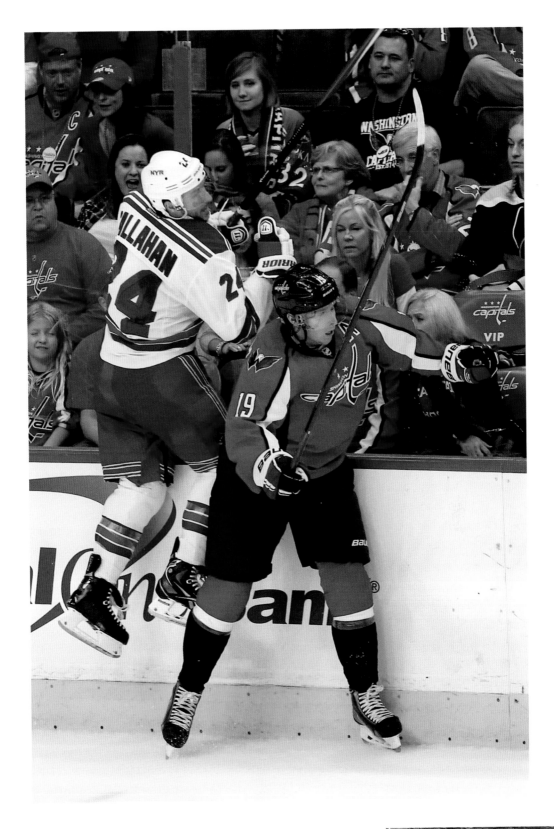

ice. When Backstrom's club season was over, he signed on once again to play at the World Championship, where Sweden finished fourth.

During the summer of 2007, Backstrom signed an entry-level NHL contract with the Capitals and stepped right into the Washington Capitals lineup at age 19. Backstrom scored 19 goals and 69 points in his first campaign, finishing second in rookie scoring and Calder Trophy voting to Chicago's Patrick Kane.

Backstrom put up a solid 14 points in his first 26 NHL games, but his rookie year caught fire when he was promoted to Washington's first line after a mid-season injury to veteran centre Michael Nylander. Backstrom used his playmaking skills to help Ovechkin produce a career year. The "Great 8" scored a career-high 65 goals and 112 points, winning the Rocket Richard Trophy, the Art Ross Trophy, the Hart Trophy, and the Lester B. Pearson Award at season's end.

Thanks in large part to the magic combination of Ovechkin and Backstrom, the Capitals improved in the standings by 24 points in 2007–08. Washington qualified for the playoffs for the first time in four seasons, and Backstrom tallied six points in the Capital's seven-game first-round loss to the Philadelphia Flyers.

At the 2008 World Championship, Backstrom chipped in seven points in nine games as Sweden skated to a fourth-place finish. Backstrom moved into the top 10 in NHL scoring in his sophomore campaign with 88 points, as Ovechkin scored 56 goals to capture his second straight Rocket Richard Trophy, Hart Trophy, and Lester B. Pearson Award.

The Capitals improved by another 14 points to finish fourth in the 2008–09 standings with 108 points, then Backstrom tallied 15 points in 14 games as the Capitals won their first playoff series since reaching the Stanley Cup finals in 1998. The team was knocked out of the post-season in the second round by the eventual champion, Pittsburgh Penguins.

The Capitals had spent a decade in the weeds, but Backstrom's arrival and Ovechkin's magic scoring touch had pulled the team into the ranks of the NHL elite. The next target: the Stanley Cup.

The plan looked promising during the 2009–10 regular season. Backstrom took another giant leap forward with career highs in goals (33), assists (68), and points (101) to finish fourth in league scoring. Even as his offensive output was peaking, Backstrom started to earn serious attention for his strong play on the other side of the puck, finishing 10th in voting for the Frank Selke Trophy, awarded to the NHL's top defensive forward.

The Capitals finished the 2009–10 season with a franchise-high 121 points, winning the Presidents' Trophy as the NHL's top regular-season team. Their high playoff hopes were dashed in the first round, however, in a seven-game loss to the Montreal Canadiens.

After failing to reach their Stanley Cup goal, Backstrom and his Capitals slid back over the next five seasons. Backstrom's personal point totals started to drop as he dealt with injuries while the Capitals developed a reputation for playoff futility, unable to push past the second round.

A personal low for Backstrom came in his second Olympic appearance in 2014. After a strong tournament for the Swedes, Backstrom was barred from playing in the gold-medal game after a drug test came back with a positive result due to an allergy medication that he had been taking. Sweden lost 3–0 to Canada and settled for the silver medal. After a long appeal process, Backstrom accepted a reprimand but was cleared of attempting to enhance his performance and was ultimately allowed to keep his silver medal.

The Capitals started to push for a championship once again after Barry Trotz took over behind the bench for the 2014–15 season. Trotz led the team to three straight regular seasons of at least 100 points and two more Presidents' Trophies in 2015–16 and 2016–17.

Backstrom's personal numbers also started increasing after he recovered from arthroscopic hip surgery during the summer of 2015. His 23 goals and 86 points during the 2016–17 regular season were his best totals since his 101-point season in 2009–10. But, once again, playoff success eluded Backstrom and the Capitals. Though Backstrom tallied 13 points in 13 games, Washington suffered another second-round defeat in seven games at the hands of their archrivals, the Pittsburgh Penguins.

Not satisfied with the disappointing end to his season, Backstrom elected to join Team Sweden at the World Championship for the first time in five years. His decision paid off as he found instant chemistry with Sweden's top line, which included Oscar Lindberg and William Nylander, the son of Backstrom's former teammate from his early years with the Capitals, who was quickly evolving into a star in his own right.

Sweden won gold. Nylander was named the tournament's most valuable player, and Backstrom collected seven points in five games — and scored the tournament-winning goal in the shootout against Canada.

As one of the highest-drafted Swiss players in NHL history, Sven Baertschi has sometimes struggled to live up to expectations. However, his talent and perseverance through injuries bode well for his future as a top-flight sniper.

Noted for his skating ability, excellent stickhandling, and quick shot, Baertschi filled the net in Swiss junior hockey with the team in Langenthal, a town of 15,000 outside Bern. Seeking to maximize his potential, the winger jumped to the WHL's Portland Winterhawks in 2010–11 and took the league by storm.

Racking up 34 goals and 85 points, Baertschi was named the runner-up to star Red Deer Rebels defenceman Matt Dumba as the rookie of the year. The Swiss forward totalled 27 points in 21 playoff games as the Winterhawks fell to the Kootenay Ice in the WHL finals.

When the Calgary Flames selected him in the first round of the draft that June, fans wondered how long it would take before he could make an impact in the NHL. The answer? Not

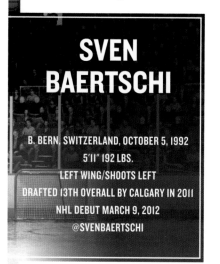

## SVEN BAERTSCHI

B. BERN, SWITZERLAND, OCTOBER 5, 1992
5'11" 192 LBS.
LEFT WING/SHOOTS LEFT
DRAFTED 13TH OVERALL BY CALGARY IN 2011
NHL DEBUT MARCH 9, 2012
@SVENBAERTSCHI

long. During a WHL sophomore season that saw him post 94 points in just 47 games, Baertschi was recalled by the injury-riddled Flames on an emergency basis. He reacted ecstatically: "I could score 10 goals in a game and it wouldn't be as good as this."

Baertschi lived up to the hype when he scored his first NHL goal on March 11, 2012, in a 4–3 victory over the Minnesota Wild. He added two more goals before being returned to the WHL. He led the playoffs with 34 points as the Winterhawks narrowly lost the league finals for the second straight year, this time to the Edmonton Oil Kings.

A neck injury limited Baertschi's productivity during his first pro season with Calgary's AHL affiliate, the Abbotsford Heat, in 2012–13. But he saw time in the NHL in 2013, chipping in three goals and 10 assists during the lockout-shortened campaign.

The Flames organization proved to be an uneasy fit for Baertschi, despite his many gifts. Just before 2013–14, Brian Burke, the team's outspoken president of hockey operations, criticized the creative young star for a lack of consistency: "Flashes of brilliance are fine if you're working in a university, but they're not much good to people in an NHL building."

When Baertschi was dealt to the Vancouver Canucks on March 2, 2015, it gave him a much-needed fresh start. He got into only three regular-season games with the Canucks but scored twice. He also saw duty in two playoff games, going pointless as Vancouver was eliminated by his old Calgary teammates in the first round. Yet he made his mark in the AHL playoffs immediately afterwards, tallying eight goals and 15 points for the Utica Devils in their run to the finals.

Baertschi finally established himself as an NHL regular in 2015–16, setting career highs with

15 goals and 13 assists in 69 games. With Vancouver, he developed on-ice chemistry and off-ice friendship with centre Bo Horvat. Daniel Sedin, who won the Art Ross Trophy with 104 points in 2011, stunned Baertschi by stating early in 2016–17 that the Swiss prodigy had more talent than he did. The team handed Baertschi a two-year, $3.7-million contract extension in June 2016.

He continued to build his popularity in Vancouver with his community involvement. Memorably, he and his girlfriend, Laura Calvert, volunteered to be locked up in the British Columbia SPCA's dog kennels to raise money and awareness for animals in need. However, ending up in Canucks coach Willie Desjardins's doghouse wasn't part of his plan for 2016–17. Baertschi was a healthy scratch for a 3–0 loss to the Washington Capitals on December 11.

Nonetheless, he responded well. Late in the season, his line with Horvat and Finnish winger Markus Granlund was the team's most effective, outshining the aging Sedin twins. And Baertschi's 18 goals and 17 assists in 69 games marked new career highs. Despite battling a concussion and another neck injury, he was a bright spot for the Canucks, even though the team finished 29th overall and fired Desjardins at the end of the year.

"It's been a little bit of a tough run," Baertschi admitted. "But everybody goes through ups and downs during the season." If healthy and happy, Baertschi still has the potential to become a dominant NHL scorer.

When Roberto Luongo compared Florida Panthers teammate Aleksander Barkov to Pavel Datsyuk early in Barkov's career, the message carried a lot of weight. After all, Luongo is one of the NHL's winningest goalies of all time and a two-time Olympic champion. "He reminds me a lot of Datsyuk, the way he skates and handles the puck and takes away the puck from other players," Luongo said. It just goes to show what Barkov has accomplished with the Florida Panthers — even before being old enough to buy a beer in the Sunshine State.

Barkov, who is of Russian and Finnish heritage, had a fine role model in his father. The senior Barkov played centre in the Soviet league in the 1980s and early '90s, including five seasons with Spartak Moscow. His son was born during his first of 10 seasons with Tappara in Tampere, and it was with that same club that Aleksander would hone his talents before arriving in the NHL.

Blessed with size and strength, Barkov attracted the attention of scouts for his creativity, confidence, and calmness under pressure. In Finland, he always played a year or two ahead of his age group. He was just 16 years old when he made his World Junior debut in 2012, potting a goal and three assists in seven games in Calgary and Edmonton. The following season, Barkov tore up the Finnish league with 21 goals and 48 points. He had a shoulder injury during Tappara's run to the finals, which required off-season surgery, but that didn't deter the Panthers' braintrust when the 2013 NHL draft came around.

Taken second overall behind speedy Canadian centre Nathan MacKinnon (Colorado Avalanche), Barkov became the second highest–drafted Finn of all time, matching goalie Kari Lehtonen in 2002 (and, later, winger Patrik Laine in 2016). Even though Barkov made the Panthers as a rookie, adjustment to life off ice in the United States wasn't always as easy for the tall centreman. For instance, he had to take his driver's licence test twice; "I failed the first time because I didn't understand the questions," he later explained.

## ALEKSANDER BARKOV

B. TAMPERE, FINLAND, SEPTEMBER 2, 1995
6'3" 213 LBS.
CENTRE/SHOOTS LEFT
DRAFTED 2ND OVERALL BY FLORIDA IN 2013
NHL DEBUT OCTOBER 3, 2013
@BARKOVSASHA95

On ice, Barkov was limited to eight goals and 16 assists in 54 games in 2013–14, as he was hobbled by two knee injuries. But it was clear that he understood the game well and could shine as both a power-play catalyst and a penalty-killer.

One highlight of his rookie season was his first career goal, in a 4–2 season-opening win over the Dallas Stars. At 18 years and 31 days old, he was the youngest player in 70 years to score in the NHL. Internationally, he had the honour of representing Finland at the 2014 Olympics in Sochi, Russia, recording one assist in two games en route to the bronze medal.

In 2014–15, Barkov's production jumped to 16 goals and 36 points in 71 games, as he saw time on Florida's top line. Luongo said Barkov was just discovering his true potential: "Once he figures

out that he can be one of the best in the league, it's going to be pretty scary." As it turned out, Florida's acquisition of an all-time legend in Jaromir Jagr from the New Jersey Devils in February helped take Barkov to another level.

The 2015–16 season saw Jagr team up with Barkov and Jonathan Huberdeau, the 2013 Calder Trophy winner. The combination of the veteran Czech's smarts with his younger linemates' speed proved to be lethal. Barkov, who received a six-year, $35.4-million contract extension, hit career highs with 28 goals and 31 assists as the Panthers won the Atlantic Division with a franchise-record 103 points.

Even though the season ended disappointingly with a six-game first-round loss to the New York Islanders, Barkov joined the Finnish national team at the World Championship for the second straight year. Playing between Laine and Florida teammate Jussi Jokinen, Barkov earned nine points as the Finns took the silver medal after a 2–0 finals loss to Canada in Moscow.

The Panthers went through turmoil in 2016–17. Off to a disappointing start, they fired head coach Gerard Gallant 22 games in. Barkov battled a bad back for much of the season, missing 21 games. His output fell to 52 points. Florida missed the playoffs for the third time in his four years with the team. But for Barkov, that should just be a brief lapse during his march to Datsyuk-like superstardom.

The path Jamie Benn took to NHL stardom was not well travelled, to say the least. Consider that he didn't play major junior hockey until after he was drafted. Benn had played provincial hockey in British Columbia, a good level to be sure, but not the same calibre as the CHL or NCAA.

Nevertheless, the Dallas Stars scouts must have seen something in him. Even though they waited until the 129th selection to call his name in the 2007 draft, they knew they'd found a gem. Benn started that fall with Kelowna; in his two years with the Rockets, he grew by leaps and bounds.

Benn had 33 goals in his first year in the WHL and 46 the next, in 2008–09. That second season was impressive on many fronts. He helped Canada win gold at the 2009 World Junior Championship and then took Kelowna to the Memorial Cup finals.

That was the end of his junior career. Big and improving seemingly daily, Benn made the Stars at camp in 2009 and never looked back. He had a strong rookie campaign, scoring 22 goals, and at season's end he went down to the AHL to help the Texas Stars advance to the Calder Cup finals.

He improved from 41 to 56 to 63 points in his first three seasons in the NHL, and after a lockout-shortened 2012–13, he was named Dallas captain during training camp in September 2013. After a strong start to the year, Benn was named to Canada's Olympic team for Sochi in February 2014. He had not been invited to the team's summer orientation camp, but GM Steve Yzerman saw the player's development and wisely added Benn to the mix.

It was a fortuitous move by Yzerman, as Benn scored the game winner in the team's first game against Norway and then scored the only goal of a tense 1–0 win over the United States in the semi-finals. Canada beat Sweden 3–0 to win gold, and the 24-year-old Benn became an Olympic champion.

His trajectory continued upwards. He again improved his goals and points totals, and he won the Art Ross Trophy in 2014–15 with 89 points, the lowest total in decades but still tops among all players.

A power forward by modern standards, Benn can skate and shoot, pass and create space, and use his body to let his stick do the talking. The only feat missing from his resume is a deep run in the Stanley Cup playoffs, but — given the team's talent and Benn's competitive nature — it's only a matter of time before he challenges for hockey's sacred trophy.

# JAMIE BENN

B. VICTORIA, BRITISH COLUMBIA,
JULY 18, 1989
6'2" 210 LBS.
LEFT WING/SHOOTS LEFT
DRAFTED 129TH OVERALL BY DALLAS IN 2007
NHL DEBUT OCTOBER 3, 2009
@JAMIEBENN14

There is something underneath the surface, something we haven't seen yet, something destined to reveal itself in good time: Sam Bennett has the skills to be a superstar in the NHL, and at just 21 years old, he has time on his side.

Leading up to the 2014 NHL Entry Draft, he was listed as the top prospect among North American players. It was a ranking well earned. Bennett had played two years of major junior, with the Kingston Frontenacs, making a case for himself as a future star.

As an OHL rookie in 2012–13, he had 18 goals and 40 points, and at the end of the season, he represented Canada at the 2013 U18 World Championship in Sochi. Bennett averaged a point per game alongside teammates such as Connor McDavid, Sam Reinhart, and Shea Theodore, and Canada won gold after beating the U.S., 3–2, in the final game.

Even before playing another game for the Frontenacs, Bennett won another gold with Canada, this time at the season-opening Ivan Hlinka Memorial Cup. He followed that win with a superior season in junior, scoring 36 goals and 91 points along with 118 penalties in minutes, a combination of skill and grit rare among teenagers.

That summer, the Flames chose him fourth overall after Florida opted to go with Aaron Ekblad first overall; Buffalo took Reinhart second; and, Edmonton went with German forward Leon Draisaitl third.

Bennett, unfortunately, succumbed to pressure. In the modern game, 18-year-old first-rounders feel it necessary to make the team at their first camp. Anything less might seem a failure. So, in September 2014, Bennett did everything possible to make the Flames, but he re-injured a shoulder that had bothered him the previous year in Kingston. Instead of a spot in the opening-night lineup, Bennett had a date with a surgeon. He missed several months after the serious procedure.

## SAM BENNETT

B. HOLLAND LANDING, ONTARIO,
JUNE 20, 1996
6'1" 186 LBS.
CENTRE/SHOOTS LEFT
DRAFTED 4TH OVERALL BY CALGARY IN 2014
NHL DEBUT APRIL 11, 2015
@SBENNETT93

When he was ready to play, the Flames wisely sent him back to junior where he played 11 games with the Frontenacs. The team was swept in the first round of the playoffs, and Bennett was recalled by Calgary to play in the team's final game of the 2014–15 regular season.

He wasted no time in making an impression, recording an assist on his first shift, on a Michael Ferland goal only 33 seconds after the opening faceoff.

Over the next two years, Bennett has shown flashes of genius but also periods of difficulty adjusting to the bigger, faster, stronger NHL. On January 13, 2016, he scored four goals in a game, the third-youngest player in league history to do so. But a more consistent, high-level game is needed from a prospect with so much talent. One great game is not enough in a league where consistent high-level play is the new norm.

A skilled winger with a strong hockey bloodline, Andre Burakovsky is a second-generation NHL player who inherited his powerful skating and top-end puck-handling skills from his father, who played 23 games with the Ottawa Senators during the 1993–94 season. Andre's uncle Mikael was also a hockey player who suited up in Germany, France, and Denmark as well as in his native Sweden. Andre's grandfather Benny served as a coach in Sweden.

Andre was born in February 1995, when his then 28-year-old father was playing with Klagenfurt AC of the Austrian league. Robert had returned to Europe after splitting his time between the Ottawa Senators and the AHL's Prince Edward Island Senators during his single season in North America.

Andre grew up primarily in Malmo, Sweden. He got his hockey start playing with the Malmo Redhawks at the U16 level, then worked his way up to the U18 team in 2010–11. One year later, at age 16, he graduated to Malmo's U20 team, where he posted 42 points in 42 games. He even saw 10 games of action at the senior men's level.

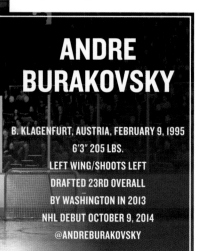

## ANDRE BURAKOVSKY

B. KLAGENFURT, AUSTRIA, FEBRUARY 9, 1995
6'3" 205 LBS.
LEFT WING/SHOOTS LEFT
DRAFTED 23RD OVERALL
BY WASHINGTON IN 2013
NHL DEBUT OCTOBER 9, 2014
@ANDREBURAKOVSKY

At the 2012 World U-17 Hockey Challenge, Burakovsky scored four goals and four assists in six games, but Sweden failed to earn a medal after falling to the United States in the tournament semi-finals. Later that spring at the IIHF's World U18 championship, Burakovsky collected three assists in six games as Sweden earned a silver medal.

In his draft year, Burakovsky was seen as an enigma. He played 43 games with Malmo's senior team, where he scored four goals and added 11 assists, but played limited minutes and, as a younger player, wasn't fully able to gain the trust of his coaches. He didn't play at the 2013 World Junior Championship; in his second World U18 tournament, however, he led his team with four goals and added an assist in five games, but Sweden was eliminated by the United States in the quarter-finals.

Headed into the 2013 draft, NHL Central Scouting slotted Burakovsky into sixth place among European skaters in its final ranking. Listed at 6'1" and 178 pounds, he was lauded for his puck-possession skills, his playmaking, and his speed. But his inconsistent season made him a question mark, and it was widely acknowledged that he'd need to add size and strength before he'd be ready to compete at the NHL level.

Projected to be chosen anywhere from 15th overall to somewhere in the second round, the Washington Capitals saw enough potential in Burakovsky to use their first pick of the draft to select him at number 23.

Washington's suggestion to help Burakovsky with his development? A year of major junior hockey in Canada. The 18-year-old signed his entry-level contract with the Capitals in September

2013, then joined the OHL's Erie Otters, where he had been the number-five pick in the import draft.

Playing on a roster that included phenom Connor McDavid, Burakovsky got plenty of ice time with the Otters, finishing his season with 41 goals and 87 points in just 57 games. He showed scoring touch in the playoffs, where he led his team with 10 goals in 14 games. He also joined Sweden at the 2014 World Junior Championship in his hometown of Malmo, where he collected seven points. The Swedes took home silver after falling 3–2 to Finland in the gold-medal game.

At his first pro training camp with the Capitals in the fall of 2014, Burakovsky proved to be a pleasant surprise, making Washington's opening-night lineup as a 19-year-old. In his first NHL game, he scored Washington's only goal in a 2–1 shootout loss to the Montreal Canadiens.

Like many skilled young players, Burakovsky has had his ups and downs during his first three NHL seasons. As a waiver-exempt player, he was assigned and recalled from the AHL's Hershey Bears six times during his rookie year. He finished the season with 22 points in 53 NHL games and seven points in 13 AHL games.

Burakovsky spent the entire 2015–16 season with the Capitals, improving to 17 goals and 38 points. Once again, his output was streaky. He scored just three goals in the first three months of the season but found his form after Christmas when he scored 10 goals and added 11 assists in 25 games during January and February.

In the playoffs, Burakovsky went cold again, contributing just one goal in 12 games. After the Capitals were ousted from the post-season by the Pittsburgh Penguins, he joined Team Sweden at the World Championship in Russia, where he contributed one goal in three games before the Swedes were eliminated in the quarter-finals.

In 2016–17, Burakovsky scored two goals in Washington's first game of the season before slumping into a 26-game scoring drought. That led Washington coach Barry Trotz to make him a healthy scratch for three games in mid-December. The player bounced back well when he returned to the lineup, though, scoring twice in his first three games.

In February 2017, a broken hand kept Burakovsky out of the lineup for an additional 15 games. After concentrated conditioning work while he was sidelined, he rejoined the Capitals late in the season in the best physical condition of his career. He ended the year with 12 goals and 35 points in 64 games. More importantly, with his legs and lungs in top form, he helped the Capitals capture their second-straight Presidents' Trophy. The next challenge was to try to shake the team's playoff curse.

When super-sniper Alexander Ovechkin struggled to score goals in the second round against the Pittsburgh Penguins, Trotz elected to move Burakovsky into Ovechkin's spot on the Capitals' top line, skating with Nicklas Backstrom and T.J. Oshie. Burakovsky responded well, scoring three goals in three games. All the same, the Capitals were eliminated.

After showing such promise in a high-intensity situation, it's hoped that in his fourth NHL season Burakovsky can fill a full-time role in Washington's "top six" and make good on his potential by scoring 25 goals or more. Now playing at 6'3" and 205 pounds, he also has the size to add a physical element to his game. In order to be stronger on pucks, he needs to come into camp in the best physical shape of his career and use his explosiveness to complement his quick release and his natural playmaking gifts.

Only 22 as he goes into the 2017–18 season, Burakovsky has shown that he has the work ethic and attitude necessary to take his game to the next level. If he can realize his potential, he'll be an important part of the Capitals offence as the team re-tools.

Burakovsky and his family are very close friends with another Swedish hockey-playing family, the Anderssons. Peter, the patriarch, had a cup of coffee in the NHL with the New York Rangers and Ottawa Senators and now coaches Andre's hometown team, the Malmo Redhawks. His older son, Calle Andersson, was drafted by the New York Rangers in 2012 and now plays in Switzerland, while younger brother Rasmus is a Calgary Flames prospect, drafted in 2015. Both generations of the two Malmo families make a point of spending time together in the off-season.

Brent Burns is a colourful guy — literally. His tattoos extend down his right arm and across his back, as well as dot his chest and legs. His personality is just as colourful. He's an animal enthusiast who has kept pet snakes and lizards. He has a zest for learning about all creatures and says he might work at a zoo when he finishes playing hockey.

With his wild mane of hair, his toothless grin, and his signature beard, it's easy to pick Burns out in a crowd. He's truly one of hockey's unique personalities.

Burns also took an unusual route to becoming a Norris Trophy winner as the NHL's best defenceman. Until he was drafted by the Minnesota Wild in 2003, he played right wing. Minor hockey for Burns began in the Ontario Minor Hockey Association, then he played with the North York Canadiens of the Metropolitan Toronto Hockey League. It took a while before Burns became the 6′5″, 230-pounder he is today. A self-described "small kid," he was selected in the third round of the OHL's bantam draft by the Brampton Battalion in 2001, and then he spent one season with the Couchiching Terriers of the Ontario Provincial Junior A Hockey League before graduating to major junior for the 2002–03 season.

## BRENT BURNS

B. BARRIE, ONTARIO, MARCH 9, 1985
6′5″ 230 LBS.
DEFENCE/SHOOTS RIGHT
DRAFTED 20TH OVERALL
BY MINNESOTA IN 2003
NHL DEBUT OCTOBER 8, 2003
@BURNZIE88

When he joined the Brampton Battalion, Burns was known as a right-winger with good hands who skated well. He started slowly but began to find his way at mid-season and finished the year with 40 points. In the playoffs, he led the Battalion with 11 points in 11 games and was voted runner-up for the OHL's most-improved player in 2002–03.

Going into the draft, NHL's Central Scouting ranked Burns at number 39 among North American skaters. It was a draft class that has become widely regarded as one of the best of all time. The Minnesota Wild surprised the experts when they selected Burns in the first round with the 20th pick. He made his first NHL fashion statement when he took to the stage in an all-white suit.

Burns surprised again when he made the Wild's opening night roster as an 18-year-old power forward, but defence-minded coach Jacques Lemaire quickly started experimenting by using him on the blue line. He played 36 games with Minnesota during the 2003–04 season, collecting one goal and six assists. He also won a silver medal as a right-winger with Team Canada at the 2004 World Junior Championship, where he tallied six assists in six games.

During the 2004–05 NHL lockout, Burns was able to hone the finer points of his game as a defenceman while spending a season with the AHL's Houston Aeros, coached by his future San Jose Sharks bench boss, Todd McLellan. He started to show the scoring touch that would come to define him, scoring 11 goals and adding 16 assists in 73 games.

When he returned to the Wild as a 20-year-old for the 2005–06 season, Burns started playing

a regular shift on defence for Lemaire. By the 2007–08 season, he had moved up to the team's top defensive pairing and became a fixture on the power play as he recorded career highs of 15 goals and 43 points.

Burns wrapped up his year with a silver medal at the World Championship, where he posted three goals and nine points and was a tournament-leading plus-14 in nine games. He returned to Team Canada at the 2010 Worlds, contributing five assists in seven games.

As he was shuffled back and forth between forward and defence, Burns was slowed by injuries over the next two seasons, but he regained his form during the 2010–11 season, reaching new career highs with 17 goals and 46 points while averaging more than 25 minutes of ice time.

When the Wild failed to qualify for the playoffs for a third straight year, Burns signed on once again with Team Canada, this time recording four points in seven games at the 2011 World Championship.

At the 2011 draft, the Wild announced that they had traded Burns to the San Jose Sharks along with a second-round draft pick, for Devin Setoguchi, Charlie Coyle, and a first-round pick. Burns joined a team that had finished first in its division for four straight years, and he was reunited with his old Houston Aeros coach, Todd McLellan.

Burns chipped in 11 goals and added 26 assists as a defenceman in his first year with the Sharks, but by 2013, McLellan had once again shifted him back to wing in an effort to maximize the impact of his offensive talents and his power forward's frame. Though he was limited to 69 games due to injuries, Burns hit a new career high of 22 goals in 2013–14 before McLellan moved him back to defence to start the 2014–15 season.

The Sharks struggled as a team, missing the playoffs for the first time in 11 seasons, but Burns took his individual game to the next level in 2014–15. He scored 17 goals, including seven on the power play, and added a stronger playmaking component to his game. His 43 assists boosted his point total to a new career high of 60, tying him for second place in scoring by NHL defencemen.

At the end of the season, Burns accepted another invite to play with Team Canada at the World Championship. With McLellan as his coach, he was named the tournament's best defenceman for the second time. He collected two goals and added nine assists as Canada went a perfect 10–0 and outscored its opponents 66–15 on the way to winning gold.

At the 2015 NHL Awards, Burns was honoured with the NHL Foundation Player Award for his work in the community. Among other charities, Burns is a strong supporter of United Heroes League, which helps children of military families play hockey, and of Folds of Honor, which provides scholarships for spouses and children of deceased military personnel.

McLellan was replaced by Peter DeBoer behind the Sharks bench to start the 2015–16 season, and Burns's game took another giant leap forward. Averaging a career high 25:52, Burns scored a league-high 27 goals and set a personal best with 75 points. Thirty of those points came on the power play, also tops in the NHL.

The Sharks returned to the playoffs after a one-year absence and made the most of their opportunity. Burns finished second overall in post-season scoring with seven goals and 24 points in 24 games. San Jose reached the Stanley Cup finals before falling to the Pittsburgh Penguins in six games.

At season's end, Burns returned to the NHL Awards, this time as a finalist for the Norris Trophy. He finished third in the voting.

After a short summer, Burns earned another championship title with Team Canada, this time at the World Cup of Hockey. He contributed three assists in six games.

The Sharks came back strong after their impressive playoff run. In 2016–17, Burns reached more personal bests with 29 goals and 76 points, setting Sharks franchise records and leading all defencemen in scoring for the first time in his career. His impressive campaign earned him his first Norris Trophy at the expense of Ottawa's Erik Karlsson. Burns was also a nominee for the Ted Lindsay Award for most valuable player voted on by members of the NHL Players' Association.

Sidney Crosby became an icon on February 28, 2010, when he scored the Golden Goal in overtime that gave Team Canada a 3–2 win over the United States and the gold medal in men's hockey at the Winter Olympics in Vancouver. For most players, that moment of hockey immortality would be career-defining, but on Crosby's résumé, it was one of many incredible accomplishments.

Crosby's latest successes are even more impressive, considering he missed a good part of two seasons with post-concussion syndrome in 2011 and 2012. At the time, it was unclear whether he'd ever play again, let alone regain the promise that led to him being dubbed "The Next One" as he prepared for the draft in 2005.

Born in Cole Harbour, Nova Scotia, Crosby's hockey blood came from his father, Troy, a former goalie whose career peaked with an appearance in the 1985 Memorial Cup. Early on, Sidney showed he was special: he did his first newspaper interview at the age of seven and was featured on CBC's *Hockey Day in Canada* as a player to watch at age 13. He put up 95 goals and 98 assists in 74 games with the midget Dartmouth Subways in 2001–02 before spending a year in the renowned hockey program at Shattuck-St. Mary's, a prep school in Minnesota.

## SIDNEY CROSBY

B. COLE HARBOUR, NOVA SCOTIA,
AUGUST 7, 1987
5'11" 200 LBS.
CENTRE/SHOOTS LEFT
DRAFTED 1ST OVERALL
BY PITTSBURGH IN 2005
NHL DEBUT OCTOBER 5, 2005

At 16, Crosby returned to Canada. Chosen first overall in the 2003 QMJHL draft by the Rimouski Océanic, he was the league's leading scorer in his rookie season with 54 goals and 135 points in 59 games and was named rookie of the year as well as most valuable player. Midway through the season, Crosby suited up for Team Canada, contributing five points in six games as Canada won a silver medal at the World Junior Championship.

In his draft year, Crosby took another giant leap forward. He won his second straight QMJHL scoring title with 66 goals and 102 assists in 2004–05 and was once again named league MVP. At his second World Juniors in 2005, he led Canada to gold as a 17-year-old.

After his standout junior career, it was a foregone conclusion that Crosby would be taken first overall at the 2005 draft. The NHL was idle during the 2004–05 season due to a labour dispute, so a new draft lottery system was put into place for the 2005 draft. The NHL used a formula that included playoff appearances from the previous three seasons and first-overall draft picks from the previous four seasons to determine the draft lottery odds. The Pittsburgh Penguins, Columbus Blue Jackets, New York Rangers, and Buffalo Sabres shared the best odds of receiving the first-overall pick at 6.3 percent each — and Pittsburgh won, setting the course that the franchise has been on ever since.

In his rookie season, Crosby moved into the home of team owner and Penguins legend Mario Lemieux in Pittsburgh. Seamlessly, "Sid the Kid" finished the season ranked sixth in

league scoring with 39 goals and 102 points and finished second in Calder Trophy voting behind Alexander Ovechkin.

At season's end, Crosby joined Team Canada's men's team at the 2006 World Championship. Canada finished fourth, but Crosby won the tournament scoring title with 16 points in nine games — the youngest ever to do so — and was named top forward.

In the 2006–07 season, at age 19, Crosby won his first Art Ross Trophy as the NHL scoring leader thanks to 36 goals and 120 points. The Penguins improved by 47 points in the standings, making the playoffs for the first time in five seasons. Crosby won the Hart Trophy as league MVP and the Lester B. Pearson trophy as MVP voted by the players. During the season, Crosby was offered the Penguins captaincy, but he held off on accepting the title until the end of the season. On May 31, 2007, he became the youngest captain in NHL history.

In January 2008, Crosby suffered a high-ankle sprain that caused him to miss 28 regular-season games, but he returned in time for the playoffs. Crosby tied Henrik Zetterberg for the post-season scoring lead with 27 points in 20 games as Pittsburgh reached the Stanley Cup finals for the first time since 1992, before falling in six games to the Detroit Red Wings.

One year later, the tables turned. After finishing third in regular-season scoring with 103 points, it was 21-year-old captain Crosby who was presented with the Stanley Cup by NHL commissioner Gary Bettman after the Penguins defeated the Red Wings in a tense seven-game finals.

The 2009–10 season was highlighted by the Olympics and Crosby's Golden Goal. He was also named a co-winner of the Rocket Richard Trophy with 51 goals.

The Penguins moved into their new arena to start the 2010–11 season, and Crosby strung together a 25-game point streak between November 5 and December 28, during which he scored 27 goals and added 24 assists. But Crosby's season ended soon afterwards when he suffered hits to the head in consecutive games — first at the 2011 Winter Classic on January 1 at Heinz Field, then in the Penguins' next game against the Tampa Bay Lightning on January 5.

The resulting concussion symptoms kept Crosby out of the lineup for the rest of the season. In 2011–12, he was limited to eight games before he felt well enough to return to the lineup full-time on March 15, 2012. Crosby finished the final 14 games of the regular season with six goals and 19 assists, then added another eight points in six playoff games.

Crosby came back fresh to start the abbreviated 48-game season after the 2012–13 lockout. With 56 points in 36 games, he was on track to win his second career scoring title when his regular season came to an abrupt halt when a slap shot from teammate Brooks Orpik broke his jaw. Crosby returned for the second game of the playoffs, wearing a special facemask. He scored 15 points in 14 games before the Penguins were eliminated by the Boston Bruins in the Eastern Conference finals. At season's end, Crosby won the Ted Lindsay Award as MVP voted by the players and finished second in Hart Trophy voting.

In 2013–14, Crosby won his second Art Ross, with 104 points, along with his second straight Ted Lindsay Award, his second Hart Trophy, and a second Olympic gold medal as captain of Team Canada.

Following a disappointing first-round loss to the New York Rangers in the 2015 playoffs, Crosby joined Canada's World Championship team for the first time since his rookie year in 2006. He captained Canada to its first gold medal since 2007 and earned a spot in the Triple Gold Club; he is the only player to have served as team captain on his Olympic–, World Championship–, and Stanley Cup–winning teams.

That win kicked off Crosby's most successful stretch of hockey to date. After replacing coach Mike Johnston with Mike Sullivan midway through the 2015–16 season, the Penguins blazed through the second half of the regular season and then won the Stanley Cup, where Crosby was named the winner of the Conn Smythe Trophy as playoff MVP.

Crosby kicked off his 2016–17 season by captaining Team Canada to victory at the World Cup of Hockey, then scored 44 regular-season goals to earn his second Rocket Richard Trophy. The Penguins became the first team in the salary-cap era to repeat as Stanley Cup champions, and number 87 became only the third player to win the Conn Smythe Trophy two years in a row. He was also a finalist for the Hart Trophy and for the Ted Lindsay Award.

Crosby joined an elite group of players as a back-to-back Conn Smythe winner. Only his team owner Mario Lemieux (1991, '92) and Philadelphia Flyers goaltender Bernie Parent (1974, '75) had previously accomplished this feat. With every passing game, the player who is no longer a kid cements his place among the greatest players ever to skate in the NHL.

When Max Domi laced up his skates on January 12, 2016, for his 42nd career NHL game, he went onto the ice and accomplished a feat that eluded his pugilistic father, Tie, over 16 NHL seasons. The younger Domi scored a hat trick. His three-goal performance helped lift the Arizona Coyotes to a 4–3 win over Edmonton.

Indeed, the athletic pedigree that Max Domi inherited from his dad is characterized by crafty playmaking and a deft scoring touch, rather than fisticuffs. The Coyotes made Domi their first-round selection in 2013, and a year later the player was given the honour of being named captain of his junior team, the London Knights.

His 2014–15 season — Domi's final year of junior — proved to be a pinnacle of teenage success. Team Canada offered him an invitation to the World Junior Championship, and Domi found instant chemistry playing on a line with Anthony Duclair and Sam Reinhart. The annual Christmastime tournament was co-hosted by Montreal and Toronto, and the Connor McDavid–led Canadians steamrolled their way to a gold medal on home ice.

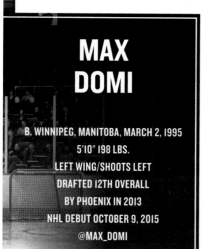

**MAX DOMI**

B. WINNIPEG, MANITOBA, MARCH 2, 1995
5'10" 198 LBS.
LEFT WING/SHOOTS LEFT
DRAFTED 12TH OVERALL
BY PHOENIX IN 2013
NHL DEBUT OCTOBER 9, 2015
@MAX_DOMI

Just under four weeks later, Domi scored the highlight-reel goal that defined his Ontario Hockey League career. As the Knights held a comfortable 4–1 lead over Sarnia, Domi got behind the Sting defence and was challenged to a foot race for a loose puck by goaltender Taylor Dupuis. Dupuis lost by a stride at the faceoff circle where an opportunistic Domi used just the right amount of force to flip the puck over the helplessly sprawled netminder and into the gaping net.

Domi registered 32 goals and 102 points in 57 regular-season games on the season, but the best was yet to come. The powerhouse Knights — led by dynamic forwards, including Domi, Mitch Marner, and Matthew Tkachuk, and goaltender Tyler Parsons — capped off an outstanding campaign with a Memorial Cup victory.

With his junior days in the rear-view mirror, Domi made the Arizona Coyotes roster out of training camp in the fall. His NHL debut was in Los Angeles on October 9, 2015, versus the Kings. The rookie did not disappoint, collecting his first career point on a first-period assist and then beating goaltender Jonathan Quick in the second period for his first NHL goal.

It became quickly evident that, even at a diminutive 5'9", Domi could maintain the scoring prowess that he displayed at the junior level while skating with the pros. By the new year, the 20-year-old had registered eight multi-point games before netting his first-ever hat trick in January.

The hapless Coyotes had a much-maligned offence, scoring a mere 209 goals on the season, the seventh-lowest total in the NHL. Defenceman Oliver Ekman-Larsson led the team with 55

points. The second rung on Arizona's scoring ladder was occupied by Domi, whose 52 points led all forwards.

At season's end, Chicago's Artemi Panarin was named the Calder Trophy winner as rookie of the year. Domi garnered enough attention to finish in sixth place in the balloting.

With the Coyotes out of the playoffs, Domi received another invitation to represent his country, this time at the senior level. The 2016 World Championship was staged in Moscow and St. Petersburg, Russia, and Domi donned a maple leaf for the second time in just under a year and a half. Domi found the back of the net just once in 10 games, but the individual statistics paled in comparison to the end result. Canada successfully defended its title at the tournament, and Domi — with another gold medal draped around his neck — got to sing his country's national anthem at the end of the championship game.

In 2016–17, Domi's sophomore season was curtailed by a hand injury sustained in a fight on December 8 against Garnet Hathaway. Surgery was required, and he missed almost two months of action. Domi played 59 games over the course of the season, finishing with only nine goals and 38 points.

Domi has become an advocate for diabetes awareness in Canada. Diagnosed with Type 1 diabetes at age 12, he persevered with the condition as he pursued his hockey career, and he even received a morale boost when he met Hall of Famer Bobby Clarke, who also lives with the disease. Domi's story serves as inspiration to those inflicted with diabetes, and the player's on-ice success is a testament to his resilience and pure skill.

Drew Doughty was raised in a soccer household, but it was clear from an early age that hockey was going to be his game. He started skating at age two and his speed was evident early; he blew away observers by skating a lap of a hockey rink in 18 seconds. That's barely five seconds from the NHL All-Star Game's fastest-skater-competition record — from a kid not yet in kindergarten!

Doughty loved hockey, but he also played soccer at a high level in his hometown of London, Ontario, until he was 15, surveying plays as they developed in front of him from his goalkeeper's box. At the same time, he was honing his hockey skills on the London Jr. Knights. He became the first player in Jr. Knights team history to have his number retired when he returned to his hometown for a banner-raising ceremony in June 2017.

Back in 2005, Doughty gave up soccer for good when started his major junior career with the Guelph Storm of the OHL. Drafted fifth overall, the 15-year-old was named to the OHL all-rookie team after scoring five goals and adding 33 assists in the regular season (and then adding 13 assists in the playoffs).

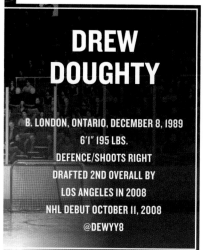

**DREW DOUGHTY**

B. LONDON, ONTARIO, DECEMBER 8, 1989
6'1" 195 LBS.
DEFENCE/SHOOTS RIGHT
DRAFTED 2ND OVERALL BY
LOS ANGELES IN 2008
NHL DEBUT OCTOBER 11, 2008
@DEWYY8

One year later, Doughty's totals increased to 21 goals and 74 points in 67 games to reach second place in scoring among defencemen. He was voted top offensive defenceman in the year-end poll of OHL coaches.

At season's end, he was named an alternate captain for Team Canada at the World U18 tournament, where he scored five points in six games as the Canadians finished fourth. The tournament was one of many opportunities for Doughty to wear the maple leaf. He also suited up for Team Ontario at the World U17 Hockey Challenge and won gold at both the 2006 Ivan Hlinka Memorial Cup and the eight-game Super Series against Team Russia in 2007.

At the 2008 World Junior Championship, Doughty was named the tournament's best defenceman. He recorded four assists in seven games to help Canada win the gold medal, but it was his skating and speed that set him apart. Indeed, it was a performance that caught the attention of NHL scouts around the league.

Back in Guelph, Doughty's offence dropped to 50 points, but he won the Max Kaminsky Trophy as the OHL's top defenceman. NHL executives were watching as the 2008 draft drew near, and Los Angeles Kings general manager Dean Lombardi got a pleasant surprise when he visited Doughty's family home in London and found a bedroom full of Los Angeles Kings memorabilia surrounding his framed Team Canada sweaters.

Not only was Doughty a lifelong Kings fan, he had phenomenal on-ice vision and a calm sense of determination that complemented his all-world skating. NHL Central Scouting listed

him third among North American skaters in their 2008 final draft rankings, but Lombardi didn't hesitate to take him second overall.

Doughty rewarded that faith by jumping straight into the Kings lineup at the beginning of the 2008–09 season — a rarity for an 18-year-old defenceman straight out of the draft. Doughty was paired with veteran Sean O'Donnell and finished the season averaging a team-high 23:49 of ice time over 81 games, chipping in six goals and adding 21 assists.

The Kings improved by eight points in the Pacific Division standings but still failed to qualify for the playoffs, so Doughty joined Canada's entry at the 2009 World Championship. He had a goal and six assists in nine games, helping the Canadians bring home the silver medal.

Doughty's strong play impressed the Hockey Canada management team that was putting together the roster for the upcoming 2010 Olympic Winter Games in Vancouver. After attending the summer orientation camp, Doughty beat out veterans such as Dion Phaneuf and Jay Bouwmeester to earn a spot on the Canadian blue line. At 20, he was the youngest player on the team when Canada defeated the United States for the gold medal.

In Los Angeles, the Kings improved their record by 22 points in 2009–10 and qualified for the playoffs for the first time in seven seasons. Doughty's 16 goals and 59 points ranked him third among all NHL defencemen and earned him third place in Norris Trophy voting as the league's best blueliner.

The Kings' fortunes got another boost in December 2011, when the team replaced Terry Murray with Darryl Sutter as head coach. In the last 49 games of the 2011–12 season, Sutter led the Kings to a 25-13-11 record, good enough to squeak into the playoffs as the eighth seed in the Western Conference.

Doughty led all defencemen with 16 points in 20 games in the playoffs as the Kings defied their low seeding to steamroll over the Vancouver Canucks, St. Louis Blues, Phoenix Coyotes, and New Jersey Devils on the way to their first Stanley Cup victory in franchise history.

Under Sutter, Doughty's role shifted. While he was still expected to put the puck in the net, his primary responsibility came as the team's top shutdown defender. That meant lower point totals but more ice time than ever, especially in critical situations.

The Kings proved that their Stanley Cup win was no fluke when they returned to the 2013 Western Conference finals before being eliminated by the eventual Cup champion Chicago Blackhawks. In 2013–14, Los Angeles got revenge by advancing past the Blackhawks at the United Center on Alec Martinez's overtime winner in Game 7, then knocking off the New York Rangers to win a second Stanley Cup in three years.

Once again, Doughty led all defencemen in playoff scoring with 18 points in 26 games, averaging 28:45 of ice time per game and finishing the playoffs with 747:33 of total ice time. That was 77 minutes more than the second-busiest player, Ryan McDonagh of the Rangers.

In February 2014, Doughty added a second Olympic gold medal to his collection. He led all

Team Canada players in Sochi, Russia, with four goals and tied Shea Weber for the team lead with six points as part of a blue-line group that gave up just three goals in the entire six-game tournament.

During the 2014–15 season, Doughty once again played more than anyone else in the NHL as his average ice time increased to a career-high 28:59 per game. His scoring also rebounded to seven goals and 46 points, and he finished the year ranked second in Norris Trophy voting as a tribute to his overall game.

One year later, Doughty doubled his goal total to 14 to go along with 37 assists and a career-best plus-24 on a Kings team with the third-best defence in the league. In what was seen as a bit of a lifetime achievement award at the ripe old age of 26, Doughty was presented with the Norris Trophy in 2016.

Before the beginning of the 2016–17 NHL season, Doughty chipped in two assists and was plus-5 as Canada took the title at the World Cup of Hockey. Adding that to his two Olympic Gold medals, two Stanley Cups, and World Junior gold, Doughty is only one World Championship gold medal away from joining the Triple Gold Club. In the meantime, he continues to be one of the premier defencemen of his era.

The list of German players who have excelled at the NHL level is short. While Marco Sturm, Jochen Hecht, Dennis Seidenberg, and Uwe Krupp are among the best skaters to ever come from Germany, Leon Draisaitl — one of the budding superstars of the Edmonton Oilers — is very quickly playing his way up the ranks.

Draisaitl's exceptional vision, uncanny instincts, and ability to find seams while making passes caught the eye of the WHL's Prince Albert Raiders, the team that chose the Cologne-born forward at the 2012 Canadian Hockey League import draft.

Although Draisaitl's parents were reluctant to let their teenaged son leave home to play hockey in rural Saskatchewan, they relented at the insistence of Raiders general manager Bruno Campese, who flew to Germany to plead his case in person.

The move paid huge dividends for all parties. Draisaitl did not look out of place in his first year of junior, 2012–13. He registered 21 goals and 58 points in 64 games to finish second in team scoring. At the international level, Germany selected the youngster for both its U20 and U18 rosters. Draisaitl was one of eight co-leaders at the U18 tournament with six assists, along with future Oilers teammate Connor McDavid.

The following season saw a dramatic increase in Draisaitl's production. In 2013–14, Draisaitl compiled an astonishing 105 points in 64 games, tying for fourth in scoring in the Western Hockey League. Once again, the surefire prospect represented Germany twice in a season, suiting up at both the U20 tournament and the senior World Championship in Minsk.

At the 2014 NHL Entry Draft in June, following the selection of consensus number-one pick Aaron Ekblad by Florida, the Buffalo Sabres chose Draisaitl's WHL rival Sam Reinhart with the second-overall pick. Edmonton gleefully scooped up Draisaitl with the number-three selection.

## LEON DRAISAITL

B. COLOGNE, GERMANY, OCTOBER 27, 1995
6'1" 216 LBS.
CENTRE/SHOOTS LEFT
DRAFTED 3RD OVERALL BY
EDMONTON IN 2014
NHL DEBUT OCTOBER 9, 2014
@DRAT_29

Although Draisaitl made his way onto the Oilers lineup out of training camp, the fresh-faced NHL rookie found himself suddenly overmatched by his opponents. Unlike in the junior ranks, where he could practically score at will, he was outmuscled in one-on-one situations and had trouble getting to, or creating, open ice.

A struggling Draisaitl compiled but nine points in 37 games before being returned to the WHL to start the new year. Shortly after his reassignment, he was traded from Prince Albert to Kelowna for the contending Rockets' playoff run.

Excelling at this lower level, Draisaitl recorded 53 points in 32 regular-season games and added 28 points in 19 playoff appearances, helping Kelowna claim the WHL title and earn a berth in the Memorial Cup. The Rockets advanced to the championship game versus Oshawa,

junior hockey supremacy hanging in the balance, only to suffer a crushing 2–1 overtime defeat.

Despite the loss, Draisaitl was awarded the Stafford Smythe Memorial Trophy as the most valuable player in the tournament. In five Memorial Cup games, Draisaitl registered four goals and seven points.

Draisaitl began the 2015–16 season with the AHL's Bakersfield Condors before being recalled to Edmonton for good in late October. He notched a surprising seven points in his first three NHL games, displaying a maturity at the pro level that had not been evident 12 months earlier. Draisaitl finished with a respectable 51 points in 72 games.

The 2016–17 season proved to be a breakout year for the burgeoning superstar. Playing in all 82 regular-season games, primarily on a line with Connor McDavid and Patrick Maroon, Draisaitl finished with 29 goals and 77 points, good for second in scoring on the surging Oilers. But it was during the playoffs — Edmonton's first post-season appearance in more than a decade — that Draisaitl rose to the occasion.

Coach Todd McLellan decided to move Draisaitl from his winger's spot on McDavid's line to a centre role alongside Milan Lucic. The move worked to perfection, particularly during Edmonton's second round matchup versus Anaheim. With the Oilers trailing three games to two in the series, Draisaitl had a game for the ages, posting a hat trick to go along with two assists in a 7–1 rout to keep Edmonton's playoff hopes alive. Although the Oilers fell in the seventh game, Draisaitl's versatility was evident. He collected an impressive 16 points in 13 post-season outings.

For good measure, Draisaitl promptly accepted an invitation to play for Germany, one of two host nations at the 2017 World Championship, and he delighted his Cologne hometown fans with two assists in three games.

After a sluggish start to his pro career, Draisaitl has proven himself to be one of the cornerstones of the Oilers franchise, one that looks to be a contender for years to come.

The jury is still out, but the question is foremost on the minds of all who speak of Jonathan Drouin — is he going to be more Alexandre Daigle or more Guy Lafleur?

The answer could go either way; he is that talented and, as of now, that enigmatic. Tampa Bay GM Steve Yzerman tried to whip him into shape but, after only modest success, decided to trade Drouin to Montreal for Mikhail Sergachyev prior to the Vegas expansion draft in late June 2017.

Drouin had a sensational junior career with the Halifax Mooseheads in the QMJHL. After a slow rookie season, he helped Canada win gold at the 2012 Ivan Hlinka Memorial Cup and exploded for 41 goals and 105 points in just 49 games in the Q's regular season.

He played at the World Juniors mid-season and led the Mooseheads to the Memorial Cup championship. Drouin was named the CHL's best player. Weeks later, Yzerman and Co. selected Drouin third overall at the 2013 NHL draft, behind only Nathan MacKinnon (Colorado) and Aleksander Barkov (Florida).

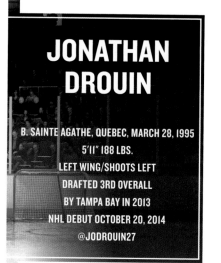

## JONATHAN DROUIN

B. SAINTE AGATHE, QUEBEC, MARCH 28, 1995
5'11" 188 LBS.
LEFT WING/SHOOTS LEFT
DRAFTED 3RD OVERALL
BY TAMPA BAY IN 2013
NHL DEBUT OCTOBER 20, 2014
@JODROUIN27

Life was good, but at Tampa's training camp that fall, it was clear to all but Drouin that he wasn't yet NHL ready. He was sent back down to junior, where he had a 108-point season and seemed poised for an NHL breakthrough.

But Drouin broke his thumb early in the 2014–15 season. When healthy, he played 70 games for the Lightning but recorded a paltry four goals. The next year, after another injury and slow start, Yzerman sent Drouin to the minors to get in some playing time and hopefully develop some much-needed confidence.

Instead, the player's agent, Allan Walsh, publicly asked for a trade. Yzerman, not one easily bullied, promised to do his best, but no solid offers materialized. Drouin refused to report to the AHL; Yzerman suspended Drouin.

After a six-week stalemate, Drouin agreed to play in the AHL and was called up at the end of the Lightning's regular season. He played well in the playoffs and had a decent 2016–17 regular season, scoring 21 goals and 53 points. However, with the impending expansion draft, Yzerman decided to trade him to the Canadiens for a prospect he wouldn't have to protect to avoid possibly losing Drouin to the Golden Knights for nothing.

In the end, things might work out well for the Quebec native, who returns home to play in 2017–18. The flip side is that he has yet to show consistent superstar play, and expectations in Montreal will be sky high. The skills are there, but is the heart and mind able to match in spirit what the stick knows is possible?

By virtue of playing on a Colorado team that has failed to advance far into the Stanley Cup play-offs in recent years, Avs forward Matt Duchene is as well known for his international successes as he is for his NHL career.

Two strong junior seasons with the Brampton Battalion put Duchene among the top prospects heading into the 2009 NHL Entry Draft. He had posted consecutive 30-goal seasons in the OHL, though never got as far as the Memorial Cup tournament.

Duchene was not big, but he had a two-way game that was impressive. Excellent offensive skills aside, he was strong defensively, a must-have in the 21st-century NHL of tight checking and low scoring. John Tavares was the first-overall selection at the 2009 draft, and when Tampa Bay chose defenceman Victor Hedman second, Duchene could not have been happier. He knew he'd go third to Colorado, the team he idolized as a kid because of Hall of Fame captain Joe Sakic.

At training camp in 2009, it was clear Duchene was ready for the NHL. This was confirmed early in the season when his play was clearly up to speed. By end of season, he had led all rookies with 55 points, one better than Tavares, and tied with Tavares for most rookie goals (21). Both men lost the Calder Trophy, though, to hulking defenceman Tyler Myers.

## MATT DUCHENE

B. HALIBURTON, ONTARIO, JANUARY 16, 1991
5'11" 195 LBS.
CENTRE/SHOOTS LEFT
DRAFTED 3RD OVERALL BY
COLORADO IN 2009
NHL DEBUT OCTOBER 1, 2009
@MATT9DUCHENE

The Avs qualified for the playoffs that year but lost to San Jose in the opening round. Duchene has watched many young stars arrive to the team, including Nathan MacKinnon and Gabriel Landeskog, but the team has made the playoffs only once since — 2014, another first-round exit.

Duchene has done his part, averaging more than 20 goals a season (including a career-best 30 in 2015–16), but the whole seems no better than the parts. This lack of playoff success has given him the chance to shine playing for Canada. Duchene first won gold in junior as part of the 2008 U18 World Championship team, and he later won back-to-back gold medals at the World Championships in 2015 and 2016.

When Tavares suffered a knee injury in Sochi, Duchene got more ice time and helped Canada win Olympic gold in 2014. He also played on the victorious Team Canada at the 2016 World Cup and won silver at the 2017 World Championship in Cologne, Germany.

Reliability at the highest level is Duchene's calling card. He can score and play defence, perhaps never making the highlight reel for a goal but also never making it for a gaffe. In the prime of his career, he is now hoping the Avs can build a winning roster so that he can perhaps not qualify to play in the World Championships — as he has six times now — because he's on a deep run to the Stanley Cup.

When you hear Jordan Eberle's name, do you think of his performance against Russia in the semi-finals of the 2009 World Junior Championship? As the Canadians aimed for their fifth-straight World Junior gold medal, Eberle kept national hopes alive by erasing a 5–4 Russian lead when he scored his second goal of the game with just 5.4 seconds left in regulation time and then followed up with what proved to be the game-winner in the shootout.

Team Canada built off Eberle's heroics with a 5–1 win over Sweden in the finals to capture that fifth-straight gold medal, tying the record that had been set by the Canadians between 1993 and 1997.

Eberle's place in national history was cemented on January 3, 2009 — perhaps the most famous U20 goal ever scored — but that World Junior performance is just one highlight of an impressive hockey career.

Born in Regina, Saskatchewan, Jordan was coached by his father, Darren, during his early years in minor hockey. His goal-scoring prowess was apparent by the time he was 10 years old. So were his unselfish tendencies: even when he has a chance to pad his stats against less-talented teams, Eberle preferred to pass the puck to his teammates, setting up other players for goals.

## JORDAN EBERLE

B. REGINA, SASKATCHEWAN, MAY 15, 1990
5'11" 184 LBS.
RIGHT WING/SHOOTS RIGHT
DRAFTED 22ND OVERALL
BY EDMONTON IN 2008
NHL DEBUT OCTOBER 7, 2010
@EBS_14

In 2004 at age 14, Eberle moved to Wilcox, Saskatchewan, to attend the fabled Athol Murray College of Notre Dame, a hockey school which has helped develop a long list of NHL notables including Wendel Clark, Russ Courtnall, Rod Brind'Amour, Vincent Lecavalier, and Brad Richards.

After recording 67 points in 27 regular-season games with Notre Dame's midget AA team, Eberle moved to Calgary with his family and joined the Calgary Buffaloes of the Alberta Midget Hockey League for the 2005–06 season. He had been drafted 126th overall in 2005 by the Regina Pats and began his major junior career with the team in 2006–07, leading the Pats with 28 goals while adding 27 assists.

In his draft year, Eberle improved to lead his team in both goals (42) and points (75), as the Pats finished first in the WHL's East Division. He won gold with Team Canada's U18 team in April and finished second in team scoring with 10 points in seven games on a squad that also featured his future Edmonton Oilers teammate Taylor Hall.

Despite his solid season, Eberle dropped from number 24 at midseason to number 33 in NHL Central Scouting's year-end rankings for the 2008 draft. As a winger, he was perceived to be less valuable than a centre or defenceman, and at 5'10" and 174 pounds, he was smaller than most of the other top prospects.

The Edmonton Oilers liked what they'd seen when they scouted Eberle and made him a first-round pick, selecting him 22nd overall — a decision that looked prescient when he went on to become a Canadian hero six months later at the World Juniors.

After being drafted, Eberle returned to Regina for a third season with the Pats, now as an alternate captain. Once again, he led his team in scoring, this time with 74 points. When the Pats failed to qualify for the playoffs, he joined the Oilers' AHL affiliate at the end of the regular season, recording nine points in nine games with the Springfield Falcons.

Eberle was one of the final cuts from the Oilers 2009–10 training camp roster, and he returned to Regina for a fourth season with the Pats, as a 19-year-old. Thanks to 25 points in his first 12 games, he was named WHL player of the month for September/October and went on to score 50 goals and 106 points to finish second overall in league scoring.

During the holiday season, Eberle re-joined Team Canada for the 2010 World Junior Championship, aiming to help Canada claim a record-setting sixth-straight gold medal. Eberle tied for the tournament lead with eight goals and was Canada's leading scorer with 13 points in six games.

In the gold-medal game, he came close to repeating history. With Canada down 5–3 in the third period, he scored twice in the last three minutes to tie the game and force overtime. This time, however, John Carlson scored for the Americans in extra time, leaving Canada to settle for silver. Regardless, Eberle was named top forward and most valuable player in the tournament.

At the end of his season with the Pats, Eberle returned to the Springfield Falcons, finishing out the regular season with 14 points in 11 games. He was a late addition to Team Canada's men's team at the World Championship, where he collected four points in four games before a quarter-finals loss. At season's end, Eberle was named the WHL and CHL player of the year.

Eberle made his NHL debut on October 7, 2010, and once again displayed his flair for the dramatic. He was named first star of the game after scoring his first career NHL goal short-handed and adding an assist in the Oilers' season-opening 4–0 win over the Calgary Flames.

Injuries limited Eberle to 69 games in his rookie season. He finished with 18 goals and 43 points, sixth among first-year players. Eberle finished 15th overall in Calder Trophy voting, well behind winner Jeff Skinner and his teammate Taylor Hall, who was ninth.

When the Oilers' season was over, Eberle embarked for the second year of what would become an almost-annual pilgrimage to the World Championship — this time scoring four goals in seven games before Canada was eliminated by Russia in the quarter-finals.

The next year with the Oilers, he hit a career high of 34 goals and 76 points in 2011–12, tying for 15th in NHL scoring. He was named to the 2012 All-Star Game and accrued a mere 10 penalty minutes in the 2011–12 season. Indeed, he finished second in voting for the Lady Byng Trophy as the NHL's most gentlemanly player.

Now established as one of the NHL's premier snipers, Eberle signed a six-year contract extension with the Oilers on August 30, 2012, that carried a salary-cap hit of $6 million per season.

Because of the lockout, he started his 2012–13 with Edmonton's AHL farm team in Oklahoma City. Though many young NHL stars were similarly forced to stay active without the NHL, Eberle was named AHL player of the month for both November and December of 2012. He was leading the league in scoring with 25 goals and 51 points in 34 games when the lockout was resolved and he was called back to the Oilers. He finished his NHL season in Edmonton with 37 points in 48 games.

In subsequent years, Eberle continued to rank among Edmonton's top goal-scorers. In 2015, he won his first gold medal at the men's World Championship in Prague, finishing second in tournament scoring with five goals and 13 points, as Canada ran the table with a 10–0 record.

After seven seasons in Edmonton, Eberle is the team's active points leader with 165 goals and 382 points in 507 games. Though he recorded his fourth-straight 20-goal season in 2016–17, his role has diminished in the two years since Todd McLellan took over behind the bench. His ice time has dropped by more than two minutes a game, and his scoring totals have taken a similar dip. Not surprisingly, he was traded — to the Islanders for Ryan Strome — in the summer of 2017, hoping for a fresh start at the Barclays Center with captain John Tavares.

Eberle has proven that he can score at any level and deliver clutch goals, but with a new team he now has to prove himself yet again.

Denmark has competed at the top level of the World Championship since 2003, but it doesn't always get respect as a top hockey nation. Thanks to the success of players like Nikolaj Ehlers of the Winnipeg Jets, that reputation is changing.

That said, Ehlers has a complicated hockey pedigree. The son of longtime European league star and Danish Hockey Hall of Famer Heinz Ehlers, he was born in Denmark but also lived in Germany when his father suited up for the Berlin Capitals. And Ehlers blossomed as a nifty winger when his father got a coaching job with Switzerland's EHC Biel.

Although diminutive, he dazzled with his blinding speed, on-ice vision, and wild array of moves. His overall athleticism was such that he even played for the Danish national junior soccer team until age 14. He made his Swiss National League debut with the senior men's club at 16, notching one goal and one assist in 11 games. He also enjoyed skating with superstars Patrick Kane and Tyler Seguin during the 2012–13 NHL lockout.

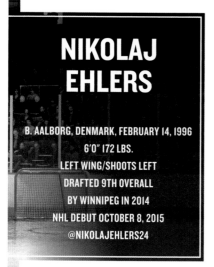

## NIKOLAJ EHLERS

B. AALBORG, DENMARK, FEBRUARY 14, 1996
6'0" 172 LBS.
LEFT WING/SHOOTS LEFT
DRAFTED 9TH OVERALL
BY WINNIPEG IN 2014
NHL DEBUT OCTOBER 8, 2015
@NIKOLAJEHLERS24

Ehlers was eager for more ice time and more responsibility. Often, Danish prospects move to Sweden to further their career, but Ehlers opted to join the Memorial Cup champion Halifax Mooseheads, which had selected him sixth overall in the 2013 CHL Import Draft. The results were spectacular.

Ehlers emerged as one of the QMJHL's most dominant and entertaining players. In his first year in Halifax, he dipsy-doodled his way to 49 goals and 104 points in 63 games, earning himself rookie of the year honours. He also had 28 playoff points before Halifax lost to the Val d'Or Foreurs in the seventh game of the conference finals. No wonder Jets GM Kevin Cheveldayoff and his scouting staff snapped him up in the first round of the NHL draft, even ahead of other blue-chip prospects like Dylan Larkin and David Pastrnak.

Ehlers speaks four languages (Danish, English, French, and German), so it wasn't hard to envision his intelligence translating to an NHL sheet of ice. But since he weighed just 160 pounds, he knew he'd have to bulk up to compete against older, stronger players. "I just want to get better," Ehlers said after the draft. "I want to improve on everything. It's hard to eat so much that you want to throw up after. I'm trying!"

The "Dashing Dane" achieved more milestones during his second QMJHL season with Halifax. He totalled 100 points in just 51 games and made the first all-star team. Even though the Mooseheads were eliminated in the second round of the playoffs, he topped the post-season with 31 points in 14 games. And over Christmas that year, he shone alongside fellow future NHLer Oliver Bjorkstrand during Denmark's first-ever top-eight finish at the World Juniors. The plucky

Danes became crowd favourites at Toronto's Air Canada Centre before falling to the host nation in the quarter-finals.

The meteoric rise of Ehlers continued in 2015–16. He made the Jets at his first NHL training camp and got off to a great start with points in eight of his first 10 games. The rookie's first goal came against New York Rangers legend Henrik Lundqvist on October 15. The Dane potted his first hat trick on January 26 when the Jets beat the Arizona Coyotes 5–2. He totalled 15 goals and 38 points in 72 games and then helped Denmark make the World Championship quarter-finals for the second time in history. It all hinted at even greater things to come.

And, as usual, Ehlers delivered. Winnipeg's addition of 18-year-old Finnish phenom Patrik Laine, the second-overall pick in 2016 who was dubbed the second coming of Alexander Ovechkin, helped in two respects. First, it lessened the spotlight and the pressure on Ehlers. Second, depending on how coach Paul Maurice configured his lines, it also gave Ehlers a bona fide sniper to set up.

Ehlers spent time alongside both Laine, who finished second in rookie scoring behind Toronto's Auston Matthews, and Mark Scheifele, whose 82 points were seventh in the league. With 25 goals and 39 assists, Ehlers achieved new career peaks. Even though the Jets missed the playoffs for the second straight year, it is obvious he remains one of the keys to long-term hockey success in the Manitoba capital.

If he had been born in a different year, Jack Eichel's hockey career might have followed a different path.

A super-skilled centre with great size, explosive acceleration, top-end fitness, and an off-the-charts hockey IQ, Eichel came into the 2015 NHL draft as the most highly touted U.S.-born prospect since Bobby Carpenter in 1981.

Following in the footsteps of Carpenter and other great American players including Patrick Kane, Phil Kessel, Mike Modano, and his future coach Phil Housley, Eichel has the talent and the desire to establish himself as one of the best American players of all time.

But Eichel came up through the minor hockey ranks at the same time as Canadian phenom Connor McDavid. Through most of his hockey life, he has felt the chill of McDavid's shadow from hundreds of miles away.

Born an hour outside of Boston in North Chelmsford, Massachusetts, Eichel developed his skills by skating on the frozen ponds of New England in the winter and playing roller hockey on the cul-de-sac outside his house in the summer. By the time he was 11, he was holding his own against players as old as 18.

## JACK EICHEL

B. NORTH CHELMSFORD, MASSACHUSETTS,
OCTOBER 28, 1996
6'2" 196 LBS.
CENTRE/SHOOTS RIGHT
DRAFTED 2ND OVERALL BY BUFFALO IN 2015
NHL DEBUT OCTOBER 8, 2015
@JACK_EICHEL11

Eichel joined the Boston Junior Bruins in 2010 at age 13 and became their captain one year later; that season, 2011–12, he scored 39 goals and added 47 assists in 36 games. He and his family also made their first visit to Boston University in 2011, exploring the prospect of NCAA hockey. Though he'd been a Boston College fan as a child, Eichel made the decision to commit to BU instead, in part because he preferred its setting in the heart of the city.

Eichel had also made a serious commitment to his fitness. His regular weight-training had him lifting 300 pounds by the time he was 16, building strength and muscularity to make it virtually impossible for him to be knocked off the puck.

In 2012, Eichel moved to Ann Arbor, Michigan, to join USA Hockey's National Team Development Program (NTDP), where he played for two years. He was named an alternate captain and scored three goals in five games as Team USA won a bronze medal at the World U17 Hockey Challenge in January. Three months later, he contributed a goal and an assist in seven games and won a silver medal at the World U18 Championship.

Though he was a full year away from being drafted, Eichel was dissatisfied with his U18 performance, particularly since McDavid had won gold and scored 10 points on his way to being named tournament MVP. Eichel used the perceived setback as motivation to train even harder, stepping up to four workouts a day.

In 2013–14, he scored 38 goals and added 49 assists in games with the NTDP. His 87 points tied him with his teammate Sonny Milano for third all-time in the NTDP record books and was named to the USHL's second all-star team.

As a 17-year-old, Eichel recorded five points in five games as the youngest player on Team USA at the 2014 World Junior Championship, then tied for the team lead with 10 points, as the United States won gold at the 2014 U18 World Championship in April.

During the two years he spent in Ann Arbor, Eichel was as committed to his studies as he was to his fitness. Online courses in the off-season allowed him to start his freshman year at Boston University when he was 17, playing a full year of NCAA hockey before he was eligible for selection by an NHL team at the 2015 draft.

At BU, Eichel's hard work began to pay major dividends. In 40 games, he tallied 26 goals and 71 points — the leading NCAA scorer in the nation. He was named most valuable player, as Boston University won the Hockey East tournament before falling to Providence in the finals of the Frozen Four. Eichel was the second freshman ever to win the Hobey Baker Award, given to the top NCAA hockey player in the country, following in the footsteps of Paul Kariya in 1993.

During the season, Eichel also served as captain for Team USA at the 2015 World Junior Championship. In May, he contributed two goals and five assists in 10 games when the U.S. men's team won the bronze medal at the 2015 World Championship in the Czech Republic.

Eichel's last chance to go head-to-head against McDavid as an amateur was at the 2015 NHL Scouting Combine, held in Buffalo three weeks before the draft. In fitness testing, Eichel showed off the impressive results of his training regime, beating McDavid's results in six of seven categories. McDavid held a slight edge in the Wingate cycling test that is designed to gauge a player's explosiveness, but Eichel came out on top in another cycling test designed to measure aerobic capacity, VO2 Max. He also scored higher than McDavid in the standing long jump, vertical jump, bench press, pull-up, and agility tests.

After a surprise win in the 2015 draft lottery, the Edmonton Oilers proceeded, as expected, to choose McDavid with the first-overall pick of the draft. Also, as expected, Eichel was taken with the second pick, by the Buffalo Sabres.

Eichel made the Sabres out of training camp and, as an 18-year-old, became the youngest scorer in team history when he logged his first goal in his first NHL game, against Craig Anderson of the Ottawa Senators. Eichel went on to record 24 goals and 32 assists in 81 games to finish second in rookie scoring behind Artemi Panarin of the Chicago Blackhawks. In the Calder Trophy race, Eichel finished fourth in voting behind Panarin, defenceman Shayne Gostisbehere of the Philadelphia Flyers, and McDavid, who missed a significant part of the season with a broken collarbone.

Before his sophomore season began, Eichel signed on with the lightning-fast Under-24 Team North America at the 2016 World Cup of Hockey, where he tallied a goal and an assist in three games. Back in Buffalo, he suffered a high-ankle sprain the day before the team's regular season began. He was out of the lineup for 21 games.

On November 29, Eichel made his 2016–17 season debut by scoring a goal and adding an assist in Buffalo's 5–4 win over the Ottawa Senators. He finished the year as the Sabres' leading scorer with 57 points in 61 games, scoring at a pace of 0.93 points per game. That ranked him in the top 15 in the NHL.

With the Sabres outside the playoff picture once the 2016–17 regular season concluded, Eichel joined Team USA for his second tour of duty at the World Championship. This time around, he chipped in five assists in eight games before a quarter-finals loss to Finland.

On the cusp of his third pro season with the Sabres, Eichel is on his way to establishing himself as a team leader, on and off the ice. He hasn't shied away from offering his opinions about what it will take to bring a winning team to Buffalo and has been active in the community. Philanthropic ventures include Tim Hortons Camp Day and a special "Shine Gold" line in his clothing collection with proceeds going to Carly's Club, which supports children and families affected by cancer at Buffalo's Roswell Park Cancer Institute.

"Exceptional" is not a word thrown around lightly in the hockey world, but it applies in more than one way to large and mobile defenceman Aaron Ekblad.

Ekblad applied for exceptional player status in 2011, asking the OHL to be allowed to play in the league at 15 years old. At that time, only one other player had been granted the request, and that was John Tavares in 2005. Ekblad's application was successful, and that fall he joined the Barrie Colts with the blessing of Hockey Canada.

Two years later, when Ekblad played for Canada at the World Junior Championship as a 17-year-old, he was nothing short of sensational. Despite his youth, he played with a maturity that belied his years. Despite the talented opposition, he played with poise. His size and speed made up for any lack of experience, and he seemed to learn by leaps and bounds with each game.

That summer, he was selected first overall in the entry draft by Florida, and in the fall, at age 18, he went to Panthers' camp, looking older and playing older than his rookie status suggested.

He made the team and earned an assist in his first game, October 9, 2014, on a Jonathan Huberdeau goal.

A forward can integrate more easily than a blueliner because he has linemates and defence to back him up. But a blueliner is the last line of defence, plays more minutes, and must face the best players from the opposition. Ekblad was a rare defenceman to make the jump from junior to the NHL without a hiccup. Midway through the year, he was named to play in the All-Star Game as an injury replacement for Erik Johnson, and by year's end, Ekblad was among the top defencemen in the league in many statistical categories.

It came as no surprise when he won the Calder Trophy, beating out Johnny Gaudreau and Mark Stone. The Panthers didn't qualify for the playoffs, and Ekblad joined Team Canada at the World Championship in Prague, Czech Republic. Once again, he was a dominant player, and Canada ran the table with a perfect 10–0 record to win gold.

After a sophomore season as impressive as his first, Ekblad was offered an eight-year, $60-million contract extension, and he accepted. The Panthers were making a clear statement that he was the core of a future Cup-contending team.

Ekblad's reputation reached a new high in the late summer of 2016 when he was named to Canada's team for the World Cup, and again he was the lynchpin on the blue line as Canada rolled to another championship.

Only 21 in his fourth NHL season, Ekblad promises to be a dominating force for the Panthers and for his country. Defencemen like him are a rare breed, and Ekblad remains an exceptional player — just as he was designated by Hockey Canada in 2011.

**AARON EKBLAD**

B. WINDSOR, ONTARIO, FEBRUARY 7, 1996
6'4" 216 LBS.
DEFENCE/SHOOTS RIGHT
DRAFTED 1ST OVERALL BY FLORIDA IN 2014
NHL DEBUT OCTOBER 9, 2014
@EKBLAD5FLA

Sometimes, a little patience goes a long way. Filip Forsberg knows this, which is why he is among the very best young players in the NHL today. The Washington Capitals know it . . . but only in hindsight after making a terrible mistake.

First off, Forsberg is his own man. He is not related to the great Peter Forsberg or any other Forsberg kicking around various leagues worldwide. Second, he showed signs of stardom early, but, unlike any other teenage flash in the pan, he has continued to develop with each year.

The young Swede grew up in the Leksand system in Sweden, content to mature at home in familiar surroundings. He had a sensational junior career internationally, winning consecutive silver medals with Sweden at the 2011 and 2012 U18 championship and three more medals at World Junior Championships: a stunning gold in 2012 and silver in both 2013 and 2014.

His maturity was such that he was considered the best European player heading into the 2012 NHL draft, but it wasn't until the 11th slot that his name was called by Washington. That year's draft was a strange one, full of missed opportunities and mistakes. None of the players selected ahead of Forsberg has gone on to show nearly the promise of the Swede, and that proves what a lottery the draft really is.

## FILIP FORSBERG

B. OSTERVALA, SWEDEN, AUGUST 13, 1994
6'1" 205 LBS.
CENTRE/SHOOTS RIGHT
DRAFTED 11TH OVERALL
BY WASHINGTON IN 2012
NHL DEBUT APRIL 14, 2013

Forsberg wasn't rushed into the NHL. He continued to play for Leksand, but on April 3, 2013, the Capitals traded him to Nashville for Martin Erat and Michael Latta. If the Caps could have a do-over, they would never have made that deal.

The Predators called him up almost immediately, and Forsberg played his first NHL game just 11 days later. The next year, he played mostly with the AHL farm team in Milwaukee; by the fall of 2014, the 20-year-old was ready to become a regular in the NHL.

In his first three seasons in the NHL, he has grown by leaps and bounds. He has played the full 82 games in each season, scoring 26, 33, and 31 goals and establishing himself as a top-six forward with the team. In the summer of 2016, Forsberg signed a new contract, a six-year deal worth $36 million, making him the core of the offence.

And, like clockwork, the team has improved its playoff performance every year. In Forsberg's first season, the team lost in the opening round. In 2015–16, the Preds lost in round two. In 2016–17, the team made it to the Cup finals for the first time in franchise history, losing to Pittsburgh in six hard-fought games.

Forsberg was integral to the team's success, scoring nine goals and 16 points in the 2017 postseason, tops on the team. Young and eager to take that final step to glory, Forsberg is poised to become one of the league's dominant players. Playing on a team that is young, with good salary-cap health, and already a Cup finalist, he's in a great place to achieve even greater glory.

Alex Galchenyuk was born in the American midwest to a family of Belarusian descent, so it should be no surprise that the Montreal Canadiens forward has an international flair to both his NHL and IIHF careers.

Blessed with good size, strong skating, and a deft touch with the puck, Galchenyuk is still looking to realize his full potential after five NHL seasons with the Canadiens — whether it's down the middle as a centreman or on left wing.

Alex's father, Alexander, was a centre himself. He started his career with Dinamo Minsk in his native Belarus before moving to Russia to join Dynamo Moscow for seven seasons. In 1982–83, Alexander, his Belarusian wife, Inna, and their daughter, Anna, set off for Wisconsin, where Alexander spent two seasons playing for the IHL's Milwaukee Admirals.

Young Alex was born in Milwaukee in 1994. His father's career led to a nomadic life. From Wisconsin, it was on to Kalamazoo, Michigan, before stops in Italy, Russia, and Switzerland.

## ALEX GALCHENYUK

B. MILWAUKEE, WISCONSIN,
FEBRUARY 12, 1994
6'1" 210 LBS.
CENTRE/SHOOTS LEFT
DRAFTED 3RD OVERALL
BY MONTREAL IN 2012
NHL DEBUT JANUARY 19, 2013
@AGALLY94

Alexander retired as a member of SKA St. Petersburg in the Russian Superleague in 2003, and the family put down its roots in Russia.

Alex dabbled in other sports, including baseball and soccer, but it was clear from an early age that hockey was in his blood. He spent most of his minor hockey years in Russia, but even as a pre-teen, he was making side trips to places such as Switzerland to squeeze in extra games when his main league's season came to an end.

By the time he was 15, Alex had set his sights on a career in the NHL, so the family returned to America. In 2009–10, he played his U16 season with the Chicago Young Americans of the Midwest Elite Hockey League, where he scored 44 goals and 87 points in just 38 games. His performance made him the top selection in the 2010 OHL draft, where he was chosen by the Sarnia Sting.

Playing with Russian sniper Nail Yakupov, who also lived with his family, Galchenyuk thrived in his first year with the Sting. He and Yakupov were both chosen for the OHL's first all-rookie team as Yakupov finished in a tie for fourth in OHL scoring with 101 points and was named CHL rookie of the year. Galchenyuk finished third in team scoring with 31 goals and 83 points.

Alexander Sr. signed on as an assistant coach in February 2011, and the Sting improved by 18 points in the league standings. Still, the team finished in fourth place in the OHL's West Division, out of a playoff spot.

Hopes were high as Galchenyuk and Yakupov headed into their draft year in 2011–12, but Alex Jr. suffered a serious knee injury in a pre-season game on September 16, tearing his ACL when

his skate caught a rut in the ice. Galchenyuk had surgery in late October and was sidelined for most of the season, returning for the last two games of the regular season and six playoff games. In front of arenas full of NHL scouts who were trying to assess his every move, Galchenyuk put up two goals and two assists in his very limited eight-game audition before the draft.

Galchenyuk was lauded for his strong pedigree, his hockey sense, and his playmaking ability — all traits that could survive a knee injury. Thus, in a 2012 draft that was perceived to be short on talented forwards, he was selected third overall by the Montreal Canadiens.

The 2012–13 NHL lockout guaranteed a return to junior for Galchenyuk, who finished his time in Sarnia on a positive note. After being named team captain to start the season, he scored 27 goals and added 34 assists in just 33 games.

In December, he travelled to Ufa, Russia, to play for his birth country, the United States, at the 2013 World Junior Championship. Galchenyuk scored two goals and added six assists in seven games for the surprise gold medal–winning American team.

Once the NHL labour dispute was settled in January 2013, Galchenyuk was immediately recalled by the Canadiens. Used mostly on the wing, Galchenyuk played all 48 games in the abbreviated season, finishing with nine goals and 27 points.

His first NHL goal came in his second game, against goaltender Scott Clemmensen of the Florida Panthers. At season's end, he was tied for fifth in rookie scoring and finished ninth in Calder Trophy voting for rookie of the year.

In the post-season, Galchenyuk chipped in three points in his first five NHL playoff games before Montreal fell to the Ottawa Senators in the first round. Echoing his childhood years, he extended his season as long as he could after the playoffs were over, joining the U.S. men's team at the 2013 World Championship. He scored twice in four games and earned a bronze medal to go along with his World Junior gold from earlier in the year.

In his second NHL season in 2013–14, Galchenyuk started to see tougher matchups on the ice, which had an impact on his performance. He managed 10 goals and 13 assists in 44 games before suffering a broken hand in January that sidelined him for six weeks. After his return, he added just eight points in 21 games before his regular season was cut short by a sprained knee with two games left on the schedule.

The knee injury sidelined Galchenyuk for most of Montreal's 2014 playoff run. He returned for Game 2 of the Eastern Conference finals against the New York Rangers and scored the biggest goal of his career to date three days later, beating Henrik Lundqvist in overtime at Madison Square Garden to give the Canadiens their first win of the series.

Once again, Galchenyuk started the 2014–15 season on the wing, but he was moved to a top-line centre role in December, playing between Max Pacioretty and Brendan Gallagher. The change paid quick dividends as Galchenyuk recorded his first career hat trick on December 14, 2014. But the celebrations wouldn't last. By mid-January, he was back on the wing.

Galchenyuk finished the season with career highs of 20 goals and 26 assists, but Canadiens fans and management were still hoping for more. The 21-year-old lived up to those expectations with a breakout campaign in 2015–16, tying with Pacioretty for the team lead with 30 goals while adding 26 assists. He still saw some time on the wing, but his best stretch of play came at the end of the season, when he moved into the top-line centre role after David Desharnais was injured. Thirteen of Galchenyuk's 30 goals came during the last 19 games of the season, while he was playing centre.

Unfortunately, Galchenyuk's coronation as the team's long-sought franchise centre was put on hold in 2016–17. He started well at centre, showing good chemistry with new arrival Alexander Radulov and collecting 23 points in his first 24 games. But he suffered another knee injury in early December that sidelined him for the better part of two months. When he returned to action, he struggled to find his form. Shuffled through the lineup during the last three months of the season, Galchenyuk finished the year with 17 goals and 44 points in 61 games.

Questions remain about whether he's better suited to play centre or wing, and what it will take for him to realize his full NHL potential, but after signing a three-year contract with the Canadiens for some $14.7 million, the Habs are betting on him to develop into a leader.

Small in stature but big on talent, Johnny Gaudreau has the speed and playmaking skills that epitomize what it takes to succeed in the modern NHL.

His success was hardly preordained. Listed at 5'6" and 137 pounds by NHL Central Scouting in his draft year in 2011, he was ranked 193rd among North American skaters when the Calgary Flames took a chance on him.

In 1998, the Flames had correctly identified a similarly talented undersized player when they signed Martin St. Louis as a free agent. Listed at 5'8", St. Louis went undrafted and didn't get his NHL opportunity until he was 23. He went on to be one of the biggest stars of his era, winning two scoring titles and a Stanley Cup as well as being named most valuable player by winning both the Hart and Lester B. Pearson trophies. Joey Mullen and Theo Fleury were other small players who had big careers in Calgary.

Born an hour away from Philadelphia in Salem, New Jersey, Gaudreau was a two-sport kid who played baseball and hockey when he was growing up. He played his minor hockey with the Philadelphia Little Flyers and spent the 2009–10 season being coached by his father, Guy, as their Gloucester Catholic High School team reached the non-public state championship game.

## JOHNNY GAUDREAU

B. SALEM, NEW JERSEY, AUGUST 13, 1993
5'9" 157 LBS.
LEFT WING/SHOOTS LEFT
DRAFTED 104TH OVERALL
BY CALGARY IN 2011
NHL DEBUT APRIL 13, 2014
@JOHNGAUDREAU03

For his senior year of high school, Gaudreau moved to Dubuque, Iowa, to join the Fighting Saints. With 36 goals and 72 points in 60 regular-season games, Gaudreau finished second in the USHL in goals and fourth in points and was named USHL rookie of the year before adding 11 points in 11 games as the Fighting Saints went on to win the league's Clark Cup.

Gaudreau arrived in St. Paul, Minnesota, for the 2011 draft with a plan to further his hockey development in the NCAA. After his name was called in the fourth round by the Calgary Flames, he prepared for a career at Boston College — a late change of plans. Gaudreau had originally signed a letter of intent with Northeastern University but switched to Boston College after Northeastern head coach Greg Cronin resigned days before the draft to become an assistant coach with the Toronto Maple Leafs.

Gaudreau quickly turned heads at BC, becoming known as "Johnny Hockey"; the pep band played Chuck Berry's "Johnny B. Goode" whenever he scored. His first-year totals of 21 goals and 44 points in 44 games placed him second in team scoring and top among all NCAA freshmen. Gaudreau was named most valuable player after Boston College won February's Beanpot Tournament, and he repeated the achievement when the Eagles won the Hockey East tournament. At the Frozen Four, Gaudreau scored a highlight-reel goal in the finals, and Boston College defeated Ferris State 4–1 to win the national title.

In his sophomore year, Gaudreau scored another 21 goals and improved to 51 points in just 35 games. He took time off during the holiday season to join Team USA at the 2013 World Junior Championship, where he led all players with seven goals and was named to the tournament all-star team as the Americans took home the gold medal.

Back in Boston, Gaudreau helped the Eagles win a fourth consecutive Beanpot title, and he won the Hockey East Player of the Year award. He was also nominated for the Hobey Baker Award as the top player in the NCAA.

Rather than make the jump to the NHL, Gaudreau opted to return to Boston for his junior year in 2014–15, partly for the opportunity to play alongside his younger brother, Matt, on the Eagles. In 40 games, Gaudreau collected 36 goals and 80 points, leading the NCAA and recording the highest single-season point total since 2003. He was named Hockey East Player of the Year for the second straight season, and on April 11, he won the coveted Hobey Baker Award.

That achievement was the perfect jumping-off point for his NHL career. Gaudreau signed an entry-level contract with the Flames that same day and was in the Calgary lineup two nights later for their regular-season finale against the Vancouver Canucks. He scored his first NHL goal on his first shot, converting a deflection past Vancouver goaltender Jacob Markstrom.

After his single-game foray into the NHL, Gaudreau joined Team USA for the 2014 World Championship. Recording two goals and eight assists for 10 points in eight games, Gaudreau finished second in scoring on his team, which was eliminated by the Czech Republic in the quarter-finals.

Gaudreau's official rookie season in Calgary began on a quiet note but didn't take long to heat up. In December 2014, he was named rookie of the month thanks to eight goals and five assists in 14 games, including his first career hat trick on December 22 against the Los Angeles Kings.

In January, Gaudreau was invited to be part of the rookie team at the NHL's All-Star Game. He was promoted to play in the main game after Sidney Crosby was forced to bow out due to injury.

On March 11, Gaudreau became the first Flames rookie since Jarome Iginla (1997–98) to score 50 points in his first NHL season. Gaudreau went on to lead all rookies with 16 points in 15 games in March and earn his second rookie of the month title.

At season's end, Gaudreau was tied with Mark Stone of the Ottawa Senators for the rookie-points lead with 64 in 80 games, including 24 goals. He was nominated for the Calder Trophy as rookie of the year but finished third in the voting behind Aaron Ekblad and Stone.

Gaudreau went on to lead the Flames in playoff scoring with nine points in 11 games in 2014–15, as his team upset the Vancouver Canucks before falling to the Anaheim Ducks.

The 2015–16 season has proven to be Gaudreau's best in the NHL so far. For the second straight year, he started the season quietly before catching fire in December — this time with a league-leading 12 goals and six assists in 13 games, which earned him the NHL's first star award for the month.

By season's end, Gaudreau had set personal bests with 30 goals and 78 points in 79 games, leading all Flames in scoring and tying for sixth place in NHL scoring with Joe Pavelski of the San Jose Sharks and Blake Wheeler of the Winnipeg Jets.

In September 2016, Gaudreau tied for the team scoring lead as part of the entertaining Under-24 Team North America at the World Cup of Hockey, tallying four points in three games. On the cusp of the new NHL season, the restricted free agent inked a new six-year contract with the Calgary Flames that carries a cap hit of $6.75 million per season.

Gaudreau's production dipped a bit in the 2016–17 season. He suffered a fractured finger in December that forced him to miss 10 games. He also found himself being checked more closely now that he had established himself as one of the NHL's top offensive threats. At season's end, he had tallied 18 goals and 61 points in 72 games, still tops on the Flames. He added two assists in the playoffs, before jetting to Europe to join Team USA for his second World Championship. This time, Gaudreau led Team USA with six goals and 11 points in eight games, but the Americans fell to Finland in the quarter-finals. His year ended on a positive note, though, as he was named winner of the Lady Byng Trophy at the NHL Awards ceremony in late June.

His nickname is "Ghost," which is a good thing because some English speakers find the French name Gostisbehere to be a mouthful. And, given his penchant for being in the middle of the action, fans are hearing the name more and more.

His father moved to Florida to play jai alai professionally, and that is how Pembroke Pines made its first contribution to the NHL register. He was born just before the Florida Panthers came into being, and as a kid he was among the thousands of die-hard fans who threw plastic rats onto the ice after Panthers' goals. Gostisbehere played youth hockey in Connecticut and then attended Union College in the ECAC.

It was during his three years with the Dutchmen that the defenceman developed into a top prospect. Not big, he skated well and had great vision. The knock was always that, as great as he was offensively, he needed to work on his game inside his own blue line.

After his freshman year in 2011–12, Gostisbehere became draft eligible. Hardly a top prospect, he was taken with the 78th-overall selection by Philadelphia. But his was not a meteoric rise. Ghost went back to Union for two more years, his time there culminating with an NCAA championship in 2014.

The final game pitted Union against Minnesota. The game was played, appropriately enough, in Philadelphia, and Gostisbehere was sensational. The Dutchmen won the game 7–4, and Ghost had a goal and two assists. More incredibly, he was on the ice for all seven goals scored and none against. The Flyers were excited by what they had discovered.

It looked like sunny days ahead, but his 2014–15 season saw an early and major setback when he tore his ACL and missed the majority of the season. He started the next year with the AHL farm team in Leigh Valley, but after being recalled, it was clear he was too good to be sent down again. Gostisbehere put together an NHL-record 15-game point-scoring streak, the longest such rookie-defenceman streak in league history, and he also scored four overtime-winning goals, the first rookie ever to do as much.

In 2015–16, he finished second in voting for the Calder Trophy, behind Artemi Panarin, and in 2016–17, he became the team's premier blueliner. Gostisbehere started that season playing for Team North America in the World Cup. In June 2017, he signed a six-year, $27-million contract extension with the Flyers, ensuring he'd be the cornerstone of a rebuilding Flyers team.

He's not big and tough in the Broad Street Bullies tradition, but he's quick and smart, and, at 24, he has many years left to improve further.

## SHAYNE GOSTISBEHERE

B. PEMBROKE PINES, FLORIDA,
APRIL 20, 1993
5'11" 180 LBS.
DEFENCE/SHOOTS LEFT
DRAFTED 78TH OVERALL
BY PHILADELPHIA IN 2012
NHL DEBUT OCTOBER 25, 2014
@S_GHOST14

In Saku Koivu's heyday with the Montreal Canadiens, the diminutive Finn was a very good NHL player, but he was a truly great international star. So far, Mikael Granlund of the Minnesota Wild has followed a similar path.

Oulun Karpat, the hockey team in Granlund's northern Finland hometown, is a frequent championship contender and has spawned stars including Reijo Ruotsalainen and Pekka Rinne. Granlund came up through Karpat's junior system but left the club after a 2009 contract dispute. He shone during his three seasons with HIFK in Helsinki.

Employing a gritty style while also showcasing his playmaking skills, Granlund recorded 40 points in his rookie season in Finland's top league and took just two penalty minutes. Thus he was named both the top rookie and the most gentlemanly player of the year.

At this time, Granlund was also a fixture on Finland's World Junior team. It wasn't a banner era for Suomi, which did not win a medal in any of Granlund's three appearances (2009, 2010, 2012). However, both he and Finland improved along the way. In his final World Junior tournament, in Calgary and Edmonton, the blue-and-white team came fourth and Granlund cracked the all-star team with 11 points in seven games.

He missed the 2011 World Juniors as a result of post-concussion syndrome, but that year also provided his most YouTube-worthy international moment. Finland beat Russia 3–0 in the World Championship semi-finals, and Granlund scored the second-period winner with a jaw-dropping, lacrosse-style goal. Outwitting defenders Dmitri Kalinin and Dmitri Kulikov, Granlund picked up the puck on the blade of his stick behind the net and flung it under the crossbar before netminder Konstantin Barulin could react. The Finns went on to hammer Sweden 6–1 in the gold-medal game in Bratislava, Slovakia, for their first gold medal since 1995.

Granlund started slowly in the lockout-abbreviated 2012–13 season, posting just two goals and six assists in 27 NHL games. He also suited up for the AHL's Houston Aeros. Noted for his competitive spirit, the Finnish rookie sometimes found himself overmatched against larger NHL opponents. Humorously, he also got the nickname "Bruce" from his Wild teammates for being slow on the uptake about Zach Parise's nickname. The American star is dubbed "Brinks" for his large bank account, but Granlund thought it was "Springs" for rocker Bruce Springsteen.

In 2013–14, Granlund tallied eight goals and 33 assists, even though injuries limited him to 63 regular-season games, but he rocked the Sochi Olympics. Finnish coach Erkka Westerlund put him on a line with the legendary 43-year-old winger Teemu Selanne, the all-time Olympic

## MIKAEL GRANLUND

B. OULU, FINLAND, FEBRUARY 26, 1992
5'10" 184 LBS.
CENTRE/SHOOTS LEFT
DRAFTED 9TH OVERALL
BY MINNESOTA IN 2010
NHL DEBUT JANUARY 19, 2013

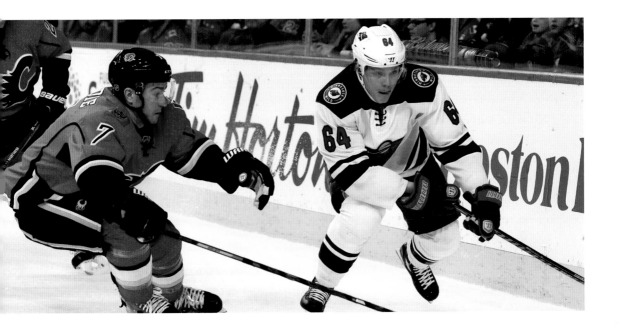

points leader who was playing in his sixth Winter Games. The two excelled in the do-or-die quarter-finals against host Russia.

Granlund set up Selanne on the rush for the second-period winner and converted a Selanne rebound in the third to round out a stunning 3–1 victory. Russian President Vladimir Putin's $50-billion party by the Black Sea was spoiled. Granlund, who made the tournament all-star team, led the Finns with seven points, and they went on to defeat USA 5–0 in the bronze-medal game.

In the 2014 NHL playoffs, his highlight was scoring the 1–0 overtime winner against the Colorado Avalanche in the opening game of the first round. He wound up with four goals and seven points; the Wild edged the Avs in seven games but lost to Chicago in six games in the second round.

Over the next two seasons, Granlund struggled to reach his offensive potential within Minnesota's defence-first system. When he made headlines, it was for oddities like tying the record for the two fastest goals by both teams in NHL history. On January 5, 2016, Nick Foligno of the Columbus Blue Jackets scored against Minnesota to make it 3–2 at 19:44 of the third period, and Granlund then shot the puck into an empty net two seconds later for a 4–2 final score.

However, Granlund's fortunes improved when interim Wild coach John Torchetti shifted him to captain Mikko Koivu's wing in 2016, a move that Bruce Boudreau, who replaced Torchetti full-time, maintained. In 2016–17, Granlund finally had his NHL breakout with 26 goals and 43 assists. The 25-year-old's 69 points tied him with mega-stars like Alexander Ovechkin, Jamie Benn, and Auston Matthews. At last, Granlund's NHL fortunes started to look as bright as his international highlights.

The son of a former Canadian Football League player, Taylor Hall fell in love with hockey as we imagine all Canadian kids did — by skating endlessly on a backyard rink. Indeed, Taylor's father was devoted to creating a sheet of ice for his young son every Alberta winter. By the time Taylor was 13 and the family had moved to Kingston, the kid was already heading towards an NHL career.

Hall scored 45 goals in just 63 games with Windsor in his first year of junior hockey and was named OHL rookie of the year. At season's end, he helped Canada win gold at the U18 World Championship in Kazan, Russia, playing alongside Jordan Eberle, Matt Duchene, and Brayden Schenn.

His next two seasons were historic. Both years, he led the Spitfires to the Memorial Cup and was named tournament MVP, the first player ever to repeat. That summer, the Edmonton Oilers drafted him first overall, and he made the Oilers at camp in the fall.

Known for his skating and ability to make plays at high speed, Hall injected much-needed offence into the Edmonton lineup. Although his rookie season ended early after he injured his ankle during a fight, he still netted 22 goals in 65 games.

The next year, he incurred a deep facial cut after a freak accident during warmup, but he still managed 27 goals in 61 games. Hall spent half of the next season in the minors, and he accepted an invitation to join Team Canada for the World Championship in Stockholm and Helsinki at the end of the year. Canada finished fifth, but this was only the start of Hall's international presence at the senior level. Hall played at the 2015 and 2016 World Championships as well, helping Canada earn back-to-back gold medals.

The Oilers were a team seemingly on the upswing. After Hall's selection in 2010, they chose first again in 2011, drafting Ryan Nugent-Hopkins, and in 2012, a third straight year, picking Nail Yakupov (unwisely, as it turned out). But for all their talented youth, the playoffs remained as elusive as ever for the team.

With the Oilers, Hall was a solid 20-goal scorer but not the superstar many had anticipated by his first-overall selection. In the summer of 2016, the Oilers traded him to New Jersey for Adam Larsson, leaving Hall devastated. He played well enough with the Devils, scoring 20 goals again, but his heart didn't seem to be in it.

Hall has the unwanted distinction of having played seven years and more than 450 regular-season games without once qualifying for the playoffs. Yet he has the speed and skill to be a contributor to a contending team, so it is likely only a matter of time before he gets a chance to play for the Stanley Cup.

# TAYLOR HALL

B. CALGARY, ALBERTA, NOVEMBER 14, 1991
6'1" 201 LBS.
LEFT WING/SHOOTS LEFT
DRAFTED 1ST OVERALL
BY EDMONTON IN 2010
NHL DEBUT OCTOBER 7, 2010
@HALLSY09

For young players growing up in the Boston area, the chance to play in the annual Beanpot Tournament is as much of an aspiration as the Memorial Cup is to Canadian kids. Indeed, Carolina Hurricanes defenceman Noah Hanifin not only attended the event every year as a youngster but eventually laced up his skates for his alma mater — Boston College — at the four-team showdown.

Even before Hanifin's collegiate days, the player was a prodigious skater, starring for both St. Sebastian's School and the Cape Cod Whalers. By the time he was selected in the second round of the 2013 QMJHL draft by the Quebec Remparts, Hanifin had already committed to the NCAA, deciding a college career better suited his development than playing in the Canadian junior system.

With superior skating ability to complement a 6'3" frame, Hanifin earned a spot with USA Hockey's National Team Development Program for the 2013–14 season. He was appointed captain of the squad, which went on to win the gold medal at the 2014 World U17 Hockey Challenge. For an encore, Hanifin also led Team USA to the top of the podium at the 2014 World U18 Championship, picking up one goal and five points in seven games.

## NOAH HANIFIN

B. BOSTON, MASSACHUSETTS,
JANUARY 25, 1997
6'3" 206 LBS.
DEFENCE/SHOOTS LEFT
DRAFTED 5TH OVERALL BY CAROLINA IN 2015
NHL DEBUT OCTOBER 8, 2015
@NHANIFIN

The following season marked Hanifin's freshman year with Boston College. At Christmastime, the defender sported the red, white, and blue emblem of his country yet again, playing at the World Junior Championship. This time, however, there would be no medal. The Americans were ousted in the quarter-finals by Russia en route to a fifth-place finish. Hanifin wound up with two assists in five games for the tournament.

One month later, in February 2015, Hanifin and the Eagles dueled against rivals Harvard, Northeastern, and Boston University at the Beanpot Tournament for the city's college bragging rights. Boston College lost a 3–2 decision to Northeastern in a semi-final matchup but then defeated Harvard by the same score — in overtime — to claim third place.

Four months later, at the NHL Entry Draft, Carolina bolstered its blue line by making Hanifin its first round, fifth-overall selection. Massachusetts was well represented in the early going: Hanifin's good friend and Boston University rival Jack Eichel had been scooped up by the Buffalo Sabres three spots earlier.

Hanifin made it onto the Hurricanes roster out of training camp at age 18. He logged over 18 minutes of ice time in his NHL debut on October 8, 2015, a 2–1 loss to Nashville. A mediocre Carolina team finished out of the playoffs in 2015–16, but Hanifin certainly did not look out of place in the NHL. He played in 79 out of 82 games and collected four goals and 22 points.

With his NHL team's season at an end, Hanifin boarded a plane bound for Moscow to join Team USA at the 2016 World Championship. At 19 years old, he was the second-youngest

player on the American roster, after phenom Auston Matthews. The United States dropped a 7–2 decision to the host Russians in the bronze-medal game and had to settle for fourth place. In 10 tournament games, Hanifin notched a goal and two assists.

In September, the World Cup of Hockey was staged in Toronto, but Hanifin missed out on an invitation. He faced stiff competition for a spot on the Team North America squad — a lineup comprising the best American and Canadian players aged 23 or younger. And, because of his age, he was ineligible to play for the veteran-laden Team USA.

Nevertheless, Hanifin rejoined the Hurricanes for his second NHL season in 2016–17. He endured a sophomore slump over the first part of the year, during which he was often relegated to the third pairing on the Carolina blue line. But when Ron Hainsey was traded to Pittsburgh, Hanifin was regularly paired with Justin Faulk as the team's top tandem.

Hanifin and Faulk complemented each other in impressive fashion, and in March, Carolina made a late-season surge for a playoff spot in the Eastern Conference. During a 13-game point streak for the Hurricanes, Hanifin logged more than 20 minutes of ice time per game — about three to four minutes above his season average.

Ultimately, Carolina fell short in its bid for the Cup chase, but Hanifin re-discovered his confidence. He finished the season with four goals and 29 points in 81 games.

With two professional seasons under his belt at age 20, Hanifin is just beginning to find his stride, and he is back on pace to fulfill the high expectations of a first-round draft pick. Big defencemen, though, tend to take longer to mature, so time is still on his side.

To understand the breeding ground from which Victor Hedman was spawned, one needs to know only one thing. The hulking defenceman was born in Ornskoldsvik, the tiny northern town that has produced a disproportionate number of superstar Swedes: the Sedins, Peter Forsberg, Markus Naslund, and Anders Hedberg, to name but a few.

As a result, Hedman developed in Modo, the local team, and he was duly scouted by NHL and Team Sweden executives. Hedman played for his country at the 2007 and 2008 U18 World Championship; in the latter year, he also played in his first of two U20 tournaments as well.

Hedman was drafted second overall by Tampa Bay at the 2009 Entry Draft, behind John Tavares, and he was a rare defenceman who made the NHL at his first camp while still a teen. Because he was tall, the learning curve was steeper for him, but the Lightning could afford to be patient because the upside to his future far outweighed any negatives.

The Lightning missed the playoffs during Hedman's first year, so he finished his season playing in his first World Championship, helping Sweden win a bronze medal. The next year, Tampa Bay went to the conference finals before losing to Boston, and Hedman was developing nicely as a physical presence and someone who could contribute to the offence as well.

## VICTOR HEDMAN

B. ORNSKOLDSVIK, SWEDEN,
DECEMBER 18, 1990
6'6" 223 LBS.
DEFENCE/SHOOTS LEFT
DRAFTED 2ND OVERALL
BY TAMPA BAY IN 2009
NHL DEBUT OCTOBER 3, 2009
@HEDS77

In 2014–15, the Lightning advanced to the Cup finals, only to lose to Chicago in six games, but Hedman was coming into his own. By 2016–17, he had become not just a physical defenceman but a leader, well rounded and in his prime. Tampa Bay gave him an eight-year, $63-million contract in the summer of 2016. Weeks later, he played for Tre Kronor at the World Cup.

Although the Lightning missed the playoffs again in 2016–17, he joined Sweden for the World Championship in Cologne and helped the team win gold thanks to a 2–1 shootout win over Canada in the final game.

As well, Hedman was a finalist for the Norris Trophy after a superb season in which he recorded 72 points in 79 games. He finished third in the voting with a respectable 728 points, behind San Jose's Brent Burns (1,437) and Ottawa's Erik Karlsson (1,292).

"I'm being put in situations to be successful," Hedman said after his career year. "I've obviously felt more comfortable on the power play. I've felt more comfortable playing that offensive role. We had to be able to produce, and that's been kind of what I expect of myself, to be one of the leaders, especially when we were in a big hole."

And as one of the best defencemen in the game today, Hedman is looking to improve his own play and inspire better play from those around him, hoping to take his game to another level and one day win the Stanley Cup.

Although Bo Horvat is still in his early 20s, it would be easy to mistake him for a seasoned NHL veteran of 30 or more, thanks to his mature demeanour and physical stature. His commitment to improvement has helped him make the transition to the NHL and endure the never-ending media spotlight in hockey-crazed Vancouver.

Family has been a big part of Horvat's journey. His father, Tim, played for the London Knights in the mid-1980s, and after tearing up local peewee and midget leagues, Bo, too, joined the famed OHL franchise. He was chosen ninth overall in the 2011 OHL draft. He attended Detroit Red Wings games as a kid, and he made another long-lasting Michigan connection when he chose the jersey No. 53. It was a tribute to goalie Ian Jenkins, a Michigan-born fellow Knights draft choice who tragically died after falling off the back of a friend's pickup truck.

Noted for his strong two-way play and faceoff skills, Horvat took big strides in his three seasons with London. Recording 30 points as a rookie under head coach Dale Hunter, he enjoyed getting to play for the 2012 Memorial Cup, even though the OHL champion Knights lost, 2–1, in the finals to the QMJHL's Shawinigan Cataractes.

## BO HORVAT

B. LONDON, ONTARIO, APRIL 5, 1995
6'0" 223 LBS.
CENTRE/SHOOTS LEFT
DRAFTED 9TH OVERALL
BY VANCOUVER IN 2013
NHL DEBUT NOVEMBER 4, 2014
@BOHORVAT

Horvat improved to 61 points in 67 games as a sophomore. But the big-bodied youngster turbo-charged his reputation as a playoff performer when he earned 23 points in 21 playoff games and the Knights repeated as OHL champs. Horvat scored a once-in-a-lifetime series winner against the Barrie Colts in Game 7 of the finals, banging a rebound past goalie Mathias Niederberger with 0.1 seconds left in regulation time for a 3–2 victory. It was his playoff-leading 16th goal, and he received the Wayne Gretzky 99 Trophy as the post-season MVP.

"It's unbelievable to win the 99 Trophy," Horvat said. "I'm humbled to have my name going on that trophy with all the other great names."

Even though London fell short again in its Memorial Cup quest, losing 2–1 to the Portland Winterhawks in the semi-finals, Horvat earned more attention with five points in five tournament games and stellar play. He was also honoured as the most sportsmanlike player after taking no penalties.

It all set the stage for the 2013 NHL Entry Draft at the Prudential Center in Newark, New Jersey, and Horvat couldn't have been selected under more dramatic circumstances. At the draft, Canucks GM Mike Gillis dealt highly touted goalie Cory Schneider to the host Devils for the ninth-overall pick, ending the speculation over whether Schneider would take starter Roberto Luongo's job. It also put pressure on Horvat to perform.

Horvat was returned to junior after his first Canucks training camp, with coach John

Tortorella telling him he needed more pace in his game. The 18-year-old didn't pout. Not only did he get 74 points in his third season with London, but he was also selected for Canada's 2014 World Junior team. He scored a goal and two assists as Canada came fourth at the tournament in Malmo, Sweden.

Debuting with the Canucks in 2014–15, Horvat proved effective in a checking role, earning 25 points as the team got 101 points under coach Willie Desjardins. Even though Vancouver was eliminated in the first round by Calgary, Horvat stepped up with a team-high four points in six playoff games.

For Horvat, 2015–16 was full of ups and downs. He was asked to shoulder more responsibility than anticipated when early season injuries to captain Henrik Sedin and Brandon Sutter forced him to play top-line minutes. Getting nine points in six games in January was his season highlight, and he finished with 40 points in a full 82-game slate. But would his minus-30 rating crush his confidence?

Far from it. Horvat's off-season training with power-skating coach Kathy McLlwain clearly bore fruit in 2016–17. While the Canucks missed the playoffs for the second straight year, Horvat recorded new career highs of 20 goals and 52 points, and he played in the NHL All-Star Game. Rushing the puck effectively and showing great chemistry with teammate and friend Sven Baertschi, the 22-year-old pivot looks like a strong candidate to become the next Canucks captain when Henrik Sedin retires.

Hockey skill, puck smarts, and blazing speed make Jonathan Huberdeau one of the NHL's most exciting players. Now in his prime, the only thing slowing him down is a Florida team seemingly stuck in neutral, but after signing a six-year, $35.4-million contract in September 2016, Huberdeau is with the Panthers for the long term.

Huberdeau started his junior career at 16 with the Saint John Sea Dogs in the QMJHL. A year later, he had established himself as one of the league's top players. As a rookie, he had just 15 goals and 35 points, but in his sophomore season he tripled those numbers to 43 goals and 105 points.

More importantly, he took the team to the Memorial Cup finals, and in the championship game he had a goal and assist to lead the Sea Dogs to a 3–1 win over Mississauga to help his team win the national championship. He was named tournament MVP for his sensational play during the post-season.

The summer of 2011, Huberdeau was selected third overall by Florida in the NHL Entry Draft, behind Ryan Nugent-Hopkins (Edmonton) and Gabriel Landeskog (Colorado). But the Panthers were not going to rush their top prospect. He returned to Saint John and also played for Canada at the 2012 World Juniors, helping his country win a bronze medal.

## JONATHAN HUBERDEAU

B. SAINT JEROME, QUEBEC, JUNE 4, 1993
6'1" 188 LBS.
LEFT WING/SHOOTS LEFT
DRAFTED 3RD OVERALL BY FLORIDA IN 2011
NHL DEBUT JANUARY 19, 2013
@JONNYHUBY11

Set to begin his NHL career in October 2012, Huberdeau had to wait. The NHL lockout delayed his debut, and he went back to New Brunswick to start a fourth year of junior. Once the NHL and players came to terms on a new deal, Huberdeau wasted no time making an impact. He scored a goal on his first shot and added two assists in a 5–1 win over Carolina; his three-point game was one of the best debuts in league history.

He went on to win the Calder Trophy in the abbreviated, 48-game regular season, but he succumbed to the dreaded sophomore slump, notching nine goals in 69 games in 2013–14. Late in the next season, he got a boost when coach Gerard Gallant put him on a line with youngster Aleksander Barkov and newly acquired greybeard Jaromir Jagr.

The year after, Huberdeau had a career-best 20 goals and 59 points, but soon after signing his massive contract extension, he suffered a terrible ankle injury, missed four months, and had only 10 goals in 31 games in 2016–17.

Entering his prime, Huberdeau has plenty more to give, but the Panthers have played only six playoff games in his five years with the team (303 games, as of summer 2017). He is an elite player, but whether he realizes his best results with the Panthers or another team remains to be seen.

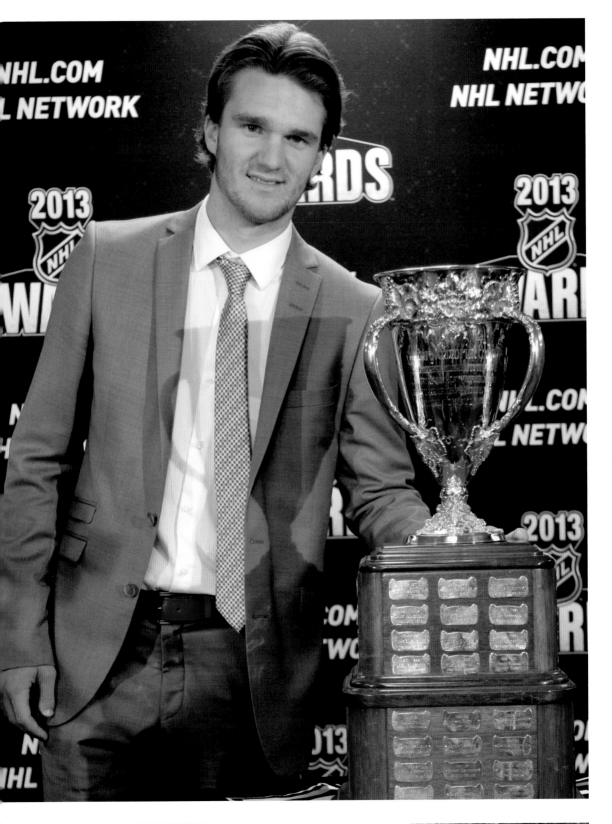

Patrick Kane's first decade as an NHL player has been one for the ages. In 10 years, he has won three Stanley Cups and a bushelful of individual awards including the Calder Trophy, Conn Smythe Trophy, Art Ross Trophy, Hart Trophy, and Ted Lindsay Award.

At 28, Kane is making a case to become the greatest American hockey player of all time. He currently leads all active U.S.-born players in points and has already climbed to number 22 on the all-time points list. He's also the first U.S.-born player ever to win the NHL scoring title and to be named league MVP.

Kane was born in Buffalo, New York, in the Irish Catholic enclave of South Buffalo. His father, Patrick Sr., owned Buffalo's largest Jeep dealership, and his grandfather, Don, was well connected in Buffalo's political circles.

The family had front-row season tickets for the Sabres at the old Memorial Auditorium. As a young child, Patrick could be spotted in the background of player photos on trading cards, and at six years old he signed his name on one of the steel beams used in the construction of Buffalo's new arena — what is now the KeyBank Center.

## PATRICK KANE

B. BUFFALO, NEW YORK, NOVEMBER 19, 1988
5'11" 177 LBS.
RIGHT WING/SHOOTS LEFT
DRAFTED 1ST OVERALL BY CHICAGO IN 2007
NHL DEBUT OCTOBER 4, 2007
@88PKANE

With his dad's encouragement and support, Patrick got serious about hockey by the age of seven. He had enough talent to go up against older players, but he was small. His parents dressed him in head-to-toe black to make him stand out and appear more threatening. He accrued 230 points in 60 games at age 11 before moving to Detroit to join the HoneyBaked AAA midget team, part of the Midwest Elite Hockey League.

Just before his 16th birthday, Kane joined USA Hockey's National Team Development program for the 2004–05 season. He led Team USA with eight points in five games in his first international tournament, the 2005 U17 Hockey Challenge.

During the 2005–06 season, Kane led the U.S. National U18 team in scoring with 102 points in 58 games. He also won gold when he led Team USA with 12 points in six games at the World U18 Championship in April — and he still had one year to go before he was eligible to be drafted.

Kane joined the London Knights of the OHL for his draft year. He had originally been drafted in the fifth round by the Knights back in 2004, but in his lone year of major junior, he led the OHL with 145 points and won the Emms Family Award as OHL rookie of the year.

Less than two months after his 18th birthday, Kane joined Team USA at the 2007 World Junior Championship. He brought home a bronze medal after finishing second in tournament scoring with nine points and being named to the all-star team — making a strong impression as a draft-eligible player.

Listed at 5'9 1/2" and 160 pounds heading into the 2007 draft, Kane was ranked second among North American skaters behind Kyle Turris. The Chicago Blackhawks were surprise draft-lottery winners after finishing 26th in the 2006–07 NHL standings. They didn't hesitate to select the diminutive Kane with their first-overall pick.

Kane made the Blackhawks out of his first training camp and immediately showed that he belonged in the NHL. With five goals and 16 points in his first 12 games, as well as a shootout winner in his second game, Kane was named rookie of the month for October 2007. He finished his first season atop the rookie scoring race with 21 goals and 72 points and won the 2008 Calder Trophy as rookie of the year, beating out Nicklas Backstrom of the Washington Capitals and teammate Jonathan Toews.

At the end of the 2007–08 season, Kane joined Team USA for the World Championship where he tied for the team lead with 10 points in seven games.

In 2008–09, Kane scored 25 goals and the rapidly improving Blackhawks qualified for the play-offs for the first time in six seasons. He led the Blackhawks with nine goals and added five assists in the post-season as the team reached the Western Conference finals for the first time since 1994–95.

The following season, Kane scored 30 goals for the first time and finished the year with 88 points, good for ninth overall in NHL scoring. The Blackhawks ended the year in first place in their division for the first time since 1992–93, then defeated the Nashville Predators, Vancouver Canucks, San Jose Sharks, and Philadelphia Flyers to win their first Stanley Cup since 1961.

Kane finished the playoffs ranked third in scoring with 28 points in 22 games. No goal was bigger than his overtime game-winner in Game 6 in Philadelphia. He became the youngest player in NHL history to score a Stanley Cup–winning overtime goal.

In February 2010, Kane contributed three goals and two assists in six games when Team USA won the silver medal at the Winter Olympics in Vancouver.

After salary-cap restrictions caused the Blackhawks to trade a number of players from their Cup-winning roster, the team took a couple of years to recover. When the league locked out its players in September 2012, Kane chose to join EHC Biel of the Swiss league, where he scored 13 goals and added 10 assists in 20 games. He was also named to the all-star team when he played at the 2012 Spengler Cup in Switzerland.

When Kane returned to North America in January, the Blackhawks went on a red-hot run through the abbreviated 48-game schedule, winning the Presidents' Trophy with a record of 36-7-5. Kane led the team and finished fifth in NHL scoring with 55 points. He led the Blackhawks with 19 playoff points and earned the Conn Smythe Trophy as post-season MVP, as Chicago won its second Stanley Cup in three seasons. Kane tied for the lead in playoff scoring with 23 points in 23 games.

Kane was named an alternate captain for Chicago to start the 2015–16 season and responded with his best year yet. Finding great chemistry with rookie Artemi Panarin and centre Artem

Anisimov, Kane tallied 16 goals and 24 assists during a 26-game point streak that lasted from October 17 until December 13. It was the longest point streak ever by a U.S.-born player and the 11th-longest in NHL history, surpassing Sidney Crosby's 25-game streak from 2010–11.

Kane was named the NHL's first star for the month of November and the third star for the month of December. He took over the lead in the NHL scoring race with a four-point night in Chicago's 4–2 home win over Edmonton on November 8 and never looked back, finishing the year with 106 points — 17 more than second-place Jamie Benn. Kane ended the season with a goal or assist on more than 45 percent of all goals scored by the Blackhawks in 2015–16. This contribution helped him win the Hart Trophy, Ted Lindsay Award, and Art Ross Trophy.

While his NHL career was peaking, Kane endured some disappointment on the international front. At the 2014 Olympics, he contributed four assists in six games but Team USA failed to return home with a medal after a 5–0 loss to Finland in the bronze-medal game. Then, at the 2016 World Cup of Hockey, the United States failed to qualify for the playoffs.

Nevertheless, Kane is in the prime of his career playing on a Chicago team that competes for the Cup with regularity. His place in history is not yet complete, but he is reaching loftier heights with each passing season. An early exit from the 2017 playoffs didn't help, but as fans know, dynasties in the 21st century game are all but impossible.

"They always say God rested on the seventh day; I think on the eighth day He created Erik Karlsson." So said Ottawa Senators general manager Pierre Dorion after his 26-year-old captain helped power his team past the Boston Bruins in the first round of the 2017 NHL playoffs.

The smooth-skating Swede has long been renowned as one of the most dynamic players in the game — a workhorse who can put up points seemingly at will and who continues to add new facets to his game.

Landsbro, Sweden, boasts a population of less than 1,500 but has raised two accomplished NHL players, Karlsson and longtime Detroit Red Wings forward Johan Franzen. Karlsson first laced up the skates as a goalie but soon switched to defence, following in the footsteps of his father, Johan.

Karlsson got his start in Swedish hockey with Sodertalje SK before moving to the Frolunda organization to start the 2007–08 season. He was named top defenceman at the 2008 U18 World Championship, where he recorded seven assists in six games before Sweden fell to the United States in the bronze-medal game.

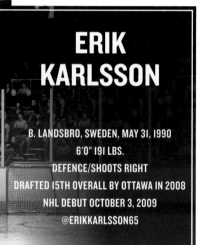

**ERIK KARLSSON**

B. LANDSBRO, SWEDEN, MAY 31, 1990
6'0" 191 LBS.
DEFENCE/SHOOTS RIGHT
DRAFTED 15TH OVERALL BY OTTAWA IN 2008
NHL DEBUT OCTOBER 3, 2009
@ERIKKARLSSON65

Though he was smaller than most of the other top defencemen in his draft class, Karlsson possessed strong skating and a calm on-ice demeanour that earned him plenty of admirers, most notably the Ottawa Senators scouting staff.

Ranked fourth among European skaters by NHL's Central Scouting heading into the 2008 draft, he was still available by the midpoint of the first round. The Senators, who were hosting the entry draft, had the 18th pick. Worried that Karlsson could get chosen before his team's turn at the podium, general manager Bryan Murray engineered a quick draft-floor trade with the Nashville Predators. By giving up a third-round pick in 2009, the Senators were able to move up three spots and select Karlsson with the 15th pick in front of their hometown fans. He was the seventh defenceman selected.

After the draft, Karlsson returned to Sweden, where he played one more year with Frolunda. At the 2009 World Junior Championship — also in Ottawa — Karlsson gave local fans a taste of things to come when he was named top defenceman, tying for the tournament-scoring lead among defencemen with nine points in seven games. He was also the top point producer on the silver-medal-winning Swedish team.

Karlsson joined the Senators at age 19 for the 2009–10 season. He played 60 games, scoring five goals and adding 21 assists while averaging just over 20 minutes of ice time per game. In the playoffs, his ice time jumped to a team-leading 25:51 per game as he tallied six points in six games in the Senators' first-round loss to the Pittsburgh Penguins. After Ottawa was eliminated, he joined Sweden's bronze-medal team at the 2010 World Championship in Cologne, Germany.

Karlsson did not receive a single vote for the Calder Trophy as NHL rookie of the year in 2010, but it wouldn't be long before he got noticed by the voters who decide the league's awards.

In his sophomore season, Karlsson improved to 13 goals and 45 points, averaging 23:30 of ice time per game, and he was selected as Ottawa's representative at the 2011 All-Star Game. The Senators missed the playoffs, and a late-season injury prevented him from joining Team Sweden for the Worlds.

The 2011–12 season marked Karlsson's arrival as one of the best defencemen in the NHL. His 78 points were a career high and 25 points better than the next highest-scoring blueliner in the league.

The 2012 All-Star Game was played in Ottawa, and the local fans jammed the ballot boxes, making Karlsson the top vote-getter among all players on a starting lineup that also included three of his Senators teammates. After a seven-game loss to the New York Rangers in the first round of the playoffs, he joined Team Sweden once again at the World Championship.

In June 2012, less than a month after his 22nd birthday, Karlsson was awarded his first Norris Trophy as the NHL's top defenceman, narrowly beating out veteran Shea Weber of the Nashville Predators.

During the 2012–13 NHL lockout, Karlsson joined Jokerit of the Finnish league, where his 34 points in 30 games made him the overall highest-scoring defenceman in the year-end standings. Upon returning to the Senators, he was leading all defencemen with six goals in 14 games when he suffered a serious injury on February 13, 2013. His Achilles tendon was lacerated by the skate of Matt Cooke of the Pittsburgh Penguins.

It was expected that Karlsson would need four to six months to recover, but he returned to the Ottawa lineup after just 10 weeks. He recorded four assists in Ottawa's last three regular-season games and led the Senators in playoff scoring with 10 points in 10 games. Ottawa won its first playoff series in six years, against the Montreal Canadiens, before falling to the Pittsburgh Penguins. On May 19, just over three months after his injury, Karlsson logged 39:48 of ice time in Ottawa's 2–1 double-overtime win in Game 3 against Pittsburgh.

Fully recovered to start the 2013–14 season, Karlsson returned to form. He was assigned the "A" as an alternate captain and once again led all NHL defencemen in scoring, cracking the 20-goal plateau for the first time as he recorded 74 points. His ice time climbed to a new high of 27:04 per game, second overall in the league.

Karlsson earned a silver medal with Team Sweden at the 2014 Olympics in Sochi, where he tied for the tournament lead in scoring with eight points and was named best defenceman.

At the beginning of the 2014–15 season, Karlsson was named Ottawa's team captain, succeeding Jason Spezza and following in the footsteps of his childhood idol, Swede Daniel Alfredsson, who housed him when he first joined the team. For the third time, he led all NHL defencemen in points with a new career high of 21 goals. The Senators went on an astonishing

23-4-4 late-season run to climb into a playoff spot. At the NHL Awards, Karlsson was awarded his second Norris Trophy.

In 2015–16, Karlsson raised the bar again, leading the league with 66 assists and finishing fourth overall in NHL scoring with 82 points, the most by a defenceman in 20 years. He also broke his idol Nicklas Lidstrom's single-season record for points by a Swedish defenceman (80 points, 2005–06). The Senators failed to qualify for the playoffs and he finished second in Norris Trophy voting, behind Drew Doughty of the Los Angeles Kings.

Karlsson tied for the lead among blueliners with four points in four games for Team Sweden at the 2016 World Cup of Hockey before logging another impressive season with the Senators. Under new coach Guy Boucher, he added a stronger defensive sensibility to his game and finished the year ranked second in the NHL with 201 blocked shots. His offence dipped only slightly, to 17 goals and 71 points, earning him a fourth Norris Trophy nomination in eight NHL seasons.

The Senators also climbed to second place in the Atlantic Division and went on an impressive playoff run that ended in overtime of Game 7 of the Eastern Conference finals against the eventual champion Pittsburgh Penguins. Though he was playing with fractured bones in his foot after being injured late in the regular season, Karlsson averaged 28:09 of ice time per game and finished as the playoffs' top-scoring defenceman with 18 points in 19 games.

Although he finished behind Brent Burns in the voting for the Norris Trophy in 2016–17, Karlsson continues to be one of the greatest all-around defencemen of this generation.

It's tough to say that Anze Kopitar is the greatest player ever to come out of Slovenia because, in truth, so few have made the leap from that tiny hockey nation to the world stage that Kopitar is without compare.

He is such a great player — and has been for more than a decade now — that his home country is beside the point. He is simply one of the most skilled hockey players in the world.

Anze's father, Matjaz, played professionally and was the boy's first coach. Anze skated on a backyard rink in Jesenice, and he developed into such a good player that Slovenia couldn't possibly develop him to his full potential. Kopitar moved to Sweden at age 16 to continue in a more challenging league, and by the time the 2005 NHL draft was at hand, he was considered the top European prospect.

In a draft in which Sidney Crosby was clearly the first-overall choice, Kopitar went 11th to Los Angeles, of course by far the highest selection for a Slovene. Kopitar spent one more year with Sodertalje in the Swedish Elite League before joining the Kings in fall 2006, a wise decision that has paid heavy dividends ever since.

**ANZE KOPITAR**

B. JESENICE, SLOVENIA, AUGUST 24, 1987
6'3" 224 LBS.
CENTRE/SHOOTS LEFT
DRAFTED 11TH OVERALL
BY LOS ANGELES IN 2005
NHL DEBUT OCTOBER 6, 2006
@ANZEKOPITAR

As a rookie, he scored 20 goals and 61 points, including two goals in his NHL debut on October 6, 2006. From day one, he has been an effective two-way player. Although he has great scoring ability, he is excellent defensively, proud of his play inside his own blue line as much as in the offensive end.

Averaging a point per game while checking the other team's best players has made Kopitar an essential part of the Kings. After just two seasons, the Kings signed Kopitar to a seven-year contract worth $47.6 million, an enormous commitment to a player who had just turned 21.

In 2009–10, Kopitar scored a career-best 34 goals and 81 points. But, although the team was improving, the playoffs seemed always too high a goal. Then, in 2011–12, everything fell into place and the Kings won the Stanley Cup. Kopitar led the playoffs in goals, assists, and points (8-12-20), and he became the first Slovene to win hockey's greatest prize.

In his 11 years with the team, Kopitar has been the top point-getter every year except his rookie season and his most recent (2016–17), and he has won the Selke Trophy as best defensive forward twice (2015, 2016). In 2015–16, he signed another contract, for eight years at $10 million a season. A year later, he was named Kings captain.

Internationally, his achievements are muted because Slovenia is a lesser hockey nation, but he did play at the 2014 Olympics and three top-level World Championships (2005, 2008, 2015). He also played on the hybrid Team Europe at the 2016 World Cup.

CSKA Moscow is Russia's most storied hockey club, producing all-time talents like Valeri Kharlamov and Vyacheslav Fetisov. Fellow CSKA alumnus Nikita Kucherov is far from equalling those names yet, but the speedy, shifty winger has already shown he's a clutch player, both internationally and in the NHL.

Kucherov learned to skate when he was five years old. He also learned self-sufficiency as a youngster, living with his grandparents when work took his parents everywhere from Uruguay to New York.

At 17, he seized the attention of scouts at the 2011 U18 World Championship in Germany when he piled up a record 21 points in just seven games as Russia took the bronze. Some observers were concerned because he'd had two shoulder surgeries. But after Tampa Bay chose Kucherov in the second round of the draft, he sparkled at the 2012 World Juniors in Calgary, helping the Russians earn silver with two goals and five assists.

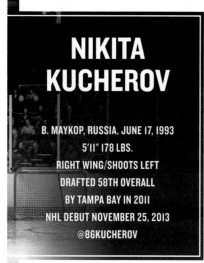

## NIKITA KUCHEROV

B. MAYKOP, RUSSIA, JUNE 17, 1993
5'11" 178 LBS.
RIGHT WING/SHOOTS LEFT
DRAFTED 58TH OVERALL
BY TAMPA BAY IN 2011
NHL DEBUT NOVEMBER 25, 2013
@86KUCHEROV

His performance on home ice at the 2013 World Juniors in Ufa was even more impressive. He saved the day with a late tying goal, won a 4–3 shootout versus Switzerland in the quarter-finals, and finished with five goals and three assists as Russia took the bronze medal.

In 2012–13, Kucherov acclimatized to North American hockey after making the jump to the QMJHL. His first team was the Quebec Remparts. Even though GM and coach Patrick Roy traded him after just 10 games, because the team was carrying too many European imports, the young Russian impressed the legendary former goalie. "He was phenomenal with the puck when he was with us for a short period of time," said Roy. "He sees the ice and his IQ is off the charts."

Kucherov's next stop was the Rouyn-Noranda Huskies, and after potting 53 points in just 27 regular-season games, he helped his new club to the third round of the playoffs, ousting the Remparts in the second round.

The following season, Kucherov cracked the Tampa Bay roster at age 20. After starting off with the AHL's Syracuse Crunch, Kucherov dazzled in his debut on November 25, 2013, against the New York Rangers, beating goalie Henrik Lundqvist on his very first shot. However, the rookie struggled to establish himself in the NHL, earning just 18 points in 52 games. Frequently a healthy scratch, he suited up for only two playoff games as Montreal swept the Lightning in the first round.

In 2014–15, Kucherov took the next step. He scored 29 goals and 65 points, leading the league with a plus-38 rating. He made an even greater impact in the playoffs. As the Lightning marched to its first Stanley Cup finals since 2004, he racked up 10 goals and 22 points, playing on the "Triplets" line with Tyler Johnson and Ondrej Palat. His clutch reputation grew with an overtime

winner against Montreal in the second round and another versus the Rangers in the Eastern Conference finals.

Even though Tampa Bay ultimately lost the Cup to Chicago, some suggested Kucherov had already supplanted two-time Rocket Richard Trophy winner and Lightning captain Steven Stamkos as the club's most dangerous weapon. Away from the rink, the Russian kept a low profile, watching TV shows like *House Hunters*, shopping for Dolce & Gabbana and Louis Vuitton clothes, and playing Xbox.

In his third NHL season, Kucherov sizzled again in the playoffs. The Lightning nearly made its second straight Stanley Cup finals appearance but fell to the eventual Cup champion Pittsburgh Penguins in Game 7 of the conference finals. But one couldn't fault Kucherov for the loss. He scored 11 goals in the run, and eight of them were either equalizers or put Tampa Bay ahead. He joined Jeremy Roenick and Evgeni Malkin as one of just three NHLers to score 10 or more goals in multiple post-seasons before age 23.

Kucherov became a bona fide NHL superstar in 2016–17. Named to the NHL All-Star Game, he scored two hat tricks during a 40-goal season that tied him with Toronto super-rookie Auston Matthews for second place behind Sidney Crosby (44). His 85 points were the NHL's fifth best. Unfortunately, the Lightning missed the playoffs, and Kucherov vented his displeasure to the Russian media. However, he finished the year on a relatively positive note, winning a bronze medal at the World Championship in Cologne, Germany. Still a youngster, he has unmistakable MVP potential.

Following in the footsteps of Finnish legend Teemu Selanne, Patrik Laine will be lighting the lamp for the Winnipeg Jets for years to come.

In his rookie season in 1992–93, Selanne set a record for NHL rookies with 76 goals and won the Calder Trophy as rookie of the year with the Jets. He went on to become the highest-scoring Finnish player of all time with 1,457 points in 1,451 NHL games.

Now, Laine is debuting the second act of this show — and it's a thriller. The 19-year-old from Tampere never saw Selanne play in Winnipeg; he was born in 1998, two years after the original Jets moved south to become the Phoenix Coyotes. Laine says his idol is Alexander Ovechkin, but he was well aware of the comparisons to Selanne when he was drafted second overall by the Jets in 2016.

In his native Finland, Laine became a superstar well before his draft day. He was a sensation by the time he was 16, and he chose to leave school so that he could focus exclusively on hockey.

When Laine started playing hockey at the age of four, he played all positions, but he especially enjoyed being a goaltender. It wasn't until he was 12, at his father's insistence, that he left the big pads behind and committed full-time to playing forward.

## PATRIK LAINE

B. TAMPERE, FINLAND, APRIL 19, 1998
6'5" 206 LBS.
RIGHT WING/SHOOTS RIGHT
DRAFTED 2ND OVERALL BY WINNIPEG IN 2016
NHL DEBUT OCTOBER 13, 2016
@PATRIKLAINE29

Given that Laine's top asset is his elite shot, he made a good choice. At the U18 World Championship in 2015, he began to make a name for himself when he tied Auston Matthews for the tournament lead with eight goals in seven games. Laine was also named to the tournament all-star team as Finland earned a silver medal.

One year later, Laine's star grew brighter when Finland emerged as the surprise winner at the 2016 World Junior Championship on home ice in Helsinki. Once again, Laine tied with Matthews for the tournament goal-scoring lead, this time with seven goals in seven games. But it was Laine who joined forces with his teammates Jesse Puljujarvi and Sebastian Aho to deliver championship gold to their countrymen.

Returning to Finnish league play after World Juniors, Laine wrapped up his regular season with 17 goals and 33 points in 46 games. He finished fifth in team scoring among players in their 20s and 30s — and he was only 17.

In the playoffs, Laine delivered spectacular highlights on a near-nightly basis. In Tappara's semi-finals against Karpat, Laine scored game-tying goals in the last minute in three consecutive games to help his team advance to the Finnish league finals. Tappara ultimately defeated Helsinki's HIFK in six games to earn the championship. Laine turned 18 on the day of Game 3 of the finals. He finished the playoffs with a league-leading 10 goals to go along with five assists in 18 games. He was awarded the Jari Kurri Trophy as playoff MVP.

After proving that he could excel in high-pressure game situations while playing against much older men, Laine was named to the Finnish team for the 2016 World Championship in Russia. Once again, he went toe-to-toe with Matthews as their June draft day drew near. Both players impressed in the tournament, but Laine's star shone brighter. He tied for the tournament lead with seven goals in 10 games, scoring three of that number on the power play with his patented shot from the top of the circle. Finland took home the silver medal, and Laine was named the tournament's most valuable player.

Laine's impressive performance at the Worlds increased the talk that perhaps he could challenge Matthews for the first pick at the 2016 draft — a ranking that had seemed like a sure thing for Matthews just a few months earlier. In the end, the Toronto Maple Leafs stayed the course and chose Matthews first, setting the stage for Laine to become the Finnish successor to Selanne in Winnipeg with the Jets.

Before their NHL careers could begin, however, Laine and Matthews squared off once again in Toronto at the 2016 World Cup of Hockey. As a U.S.-born player, Matthews suited up for the Under-24 Team North American squad, while 18-year-old Laine, the youngest player in the tournament, skated for Team Finland. Neither player reached the playoff round.

In October, Laine made his NHL debut, scoring his first goal and recording his first assist in his first game — a 5–4 overtime win over the Carolina Hurricanes.

Just three games later, Laine and Matthews met for the first time as NHL opponents. Laine chose the occasion to tally his first NHL hat trick when he scored the overtime game-winner in a 5–4 victory, lifting Jets fans out of their seats with his natural scoring ability.

Showing a propensity for scoring in bunches, Laine recorded his second hat trick just 10 games later, once again scoring the game-winning goal in an 8–2 victory over the Dallas Stars on November 8.

As the calendar flipped to 2017, Laine sat at the top of the rookie scoring race with 19 goals and 31 points — one goal and one point ahead of Matthews. The Finn hit the 20-goal mark on January 3 against the Tampa Bay Lightning, but he missed eight games that month when he suffered a concussion from an open-ice hit by Buffalo Sabres defenceman Jake McCabe on January 8.

Laine returned to action on January 24, just days before taking to the ice as the Jets' representative at the 2017 All-Star Game. In the skills competition, Laine finished second to three-time champion Shea Weber in the hardest-shot competition with a blast of 101.7 miles per hour. He went on to finish three-tenths of a second behind Connor McDavid in the fastest skater competition, with a time of 13.420 seconds.

In February, Laine had his best month yet. He was named rookie of the month thanks to eight goals and seven assists in 11 games, which helped him maintain a one-point edge over Matthews in the rookie scoring race.

On February 14, Laine became the first rookie to score three hat tricks in a season since

Selanne (five) and Eric Lindros (three) in 1992–93. Laine is the only player in NHL history to score three hat tricks before his 19th birthday.

On February 20, Laine scored his 30th goal of the year against the Maple Leafs to set a new Jets franchise record for rookie scoring. Selanne's old record of 76 goals, of course, is now part of the Arizona Coyotes' history, while Laine's achievement tops all current Jets and members of the defunct Atlanta Thrashers. (The old rookie record was set by Ilya Kovalchuk in 2001–02.)

Laine also became only the third player in the salary-cap era to reach the 30-goal plateau as an 18-year-old, following in the footsteps of Sidney Crosby (39 goals, 2005–06) and Jeff Skinner (31 goals, 2010–11). At season's end, his 36 goals ranked him seventh all-time among 18-year-olds, behind leader Wayne Gretzky (51 goals, 1979–80) and another great from the original Jets, Dale Hawerchuk (45 goals, 1981–82).

Laine's 36 goals and 64 points in 2016–17 ultimately landed him second to Matthews in the rookie scoring race. He led the Jets in goals and finished in a tie for third in team scoring but fell short of the franchise record of 67 points by a rookie, set by Dany Heatley in 2001–02. Laine was nominated for the Calder Trophy as rookie of the year but finished behind Matthews, who won in a landslide, taking 164 of 167 first-place votes.

No matter. Laine and his shot will be front and centre in the NHL for a long, long time, much to the delight of Jets fans across Manitoba. His size, his confidence, and his incredible stick speed will ensure as much.

It's crazy to think that a tiny town (Cole Harbour) in a tiny province (Nova Scotia) could yield not one but two world-class NHLers, but that's what has happened. First Sidney Crosby (born 1987) and, eight years later, Nathan MacKinnon.

And, like his idol Crosby, MacKinnon starred in local minor hockey and then went to Shattuck-St. Mary's in Faribault, Minnesota, to continue to develop in relative obscurity. However, MacKinnon played two years at the prep high school before joining the QMJHL, whereas Crosby played just one year before playing in the Q. Both were just 16 when they began their junior careers, Crosby with Rimouski and MacKinnon with Halifax.

MacKinnon did one thing in the Q that Crosby did not: win the Memorial Cup. In 2011–12, his rookie season, MacKinnon had 31 goals and 78 points in 58 games, but the Mooseheads didn't make it to the Memorial Cup. The 2012–13 season, though, was different. Now 17, MacKinnon was named to Canada's team for the Ivan Hlinka Memorial Cup at the start of the year, helping the team win gold.

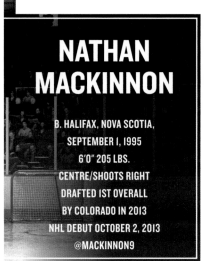

## NATHAN MACKINNON

B. HALIFAX, NOVA SCOTIA,
SEPTEMBER 1, 1995
6'0" 205 LBS.
CENTRE/SHOOTS RIGHT
DRAFTED 1ST OVERALL
BY COLORADO IN 2013
NHL DEBUT OCTOBER 2, 2013
@MACKINNON9

At mid-season, he played for Canada at the World Juniors. At the end of the year, he took Halifax to the Memorial Cup, scoring a hat trick in the championship game to give the team a 6–4 win over the Portland Winterhawks. He was also named tournament MVP.

That summer, MacKinnon was drafted first overall by Colorado at the NHL Entry Draft, just as Crosby had been eight years earlier. He made the Avs at training camp in September 2013, and in his first NHL game he collected two assists in a 6–1 win over Anaheim. His career was off and running.

In his rookie season, MacKinnon set two "youngest to" records. In January 2014, he was the youngest player in league history to record back-to-back two-goal games, and later he put together a 13-game point-scoring streak, the longest such streak by an 18-year-old.

MacKinnon finished his first NHL season with 24 goals and 63 points and won the Calder Trophy. Since then, he has yet to equal or improve upon those numbers, and his career has stalled as the Avs have struggled. He's a player full of talent without a coach to nurture and develop individual skills to produce a better team. The Avs qualified for the playoffs in MacKinnon's first season, losing in the opening round, and have yet to return to the post-season since.

Still, MacKinnon has performed in a way that makes him an elite player. He has size and speed and a great shot, and he has proven himself on the international stage. MacKinnon won a gold medal with Canada at the 2015 World Championship, and a silver in 2017, and in 2016 he was one of the stars of the young Team North America at the World Cup. Indeed, he scored arguably the best goal of the event, undressing Henrik Lundqvist from in close in overtime against Sweden. To be sure, his is a talent that few in the high-speed modern NHL can match.

Let's get straight to the point: Evgeni Malkin and Sidney Crosby have formed the top one-two punch down the middle in the NHL for the last 11 seasons with the Pittsburgh Penguins.

The 2004 draft was the Year of the Russians — the only time that Russian players were the top two picks. Alexander Ovechkin went first to the Washington Capitals, followed by his countryman Malkin. As well, Alexander Radulov was chosen 15th overall.

Malkin is a native of Magnitogorsk, a city of 400,000 located more than a thousand miles east of Moscow. His father, Vladimir, had played with the hometown hockey team in Magnitogorsk, Metallurg, and Evgeni followed in his father's footsteps, joining the organization as a junior. At 16, he won a bronze medal at the 2003 World U18 Championship in Yaroslavl, Russia. He joined the senior Metallurg team in the Russian Superleague for the 2003–04 season.

He recorded 12 points in 34 league games his draft year and won his first gold medal with Russia in the 2004 U18 tournament in April. Earlier that year, he had recorded five points in six games as Russia finished fifth at the 2004 World Junior Championship.

**EVGENI MALKIN**

B. MAGNITOGORSK, SOVIET UNION (RUSSIA), JULY 31, 1986
6'3" 195 LBS.
CENTRE/SHOOTS LEFT
DRAFTED 2ND OVERALL
BY PITTSBURGH IN 2004
NHL DEBUT OCTOBER 18, 2006

Since Magnitogorsk is home to the largest iron and steel works in Russia, it was fitting that Malkin was drafted by Pittsburgh, America's Steel City. The start of his North American career was delayed by the 2004–05 NHL lockout and an international transfer dispute that kept him in Russia through the 2005–06 season.

Malkin posted 12 goals and 32 points in 52 games with Metallurg in 2004–05, then improved to 21-26-47 in 46 games in 2005–06 as his team finished first overall in the Superleague. He then added 15 points in 11 playoff games.

He also stayed busy on the international front. Malkin won silver medals with Russia at both the 2005 and 2006 World Junior Championships and bronze at the 2005 World Championship. But he failed to bring home a medal at either the 2006 Worlds (Russia finished fifth) or the 2006 Olympics (fourth).

Malkin finally arrived in Pittsburgh at the beginning of the 2006–07 season. After dislocating his shoulder in his first pre-season game, he was forced to miss Pittsburgh's first four regular-season games to recover from the injury.

When he finally made his regular-season debut, Malkin quickly established himself as an elite talent alongside his teammate Sidney Crosby. He scored seven goals and added four assists in his first six games with the Penguins and was named the NHL's rookie of the month for October 2006.

At the end of his rookie season, Malkin led all first-year players with 33 goals and 85 points and was awarded the Calder Trophy. The Penguins also improved by 47 points in the regular-season

standings and made the playoffs for the first time in five years, kicking off a string of 11 consecutive post-season appearances that is now the longest active streak in the NHL.

After a first-round loss in the 2007 playoffs, Malkin joined Team Russia for a third consecutive World Championship appearance. He posted 10 points in nine games and won a bronze medal in Moscow.

In 2007–08, Malkin improved to 47 goals and 106 points with the Penguins, finishing second overall in NHL scoring behind Ovechkin. In his second NHL season, he finished second in Hart Trophy voting for the NHL's most valuable player, also behind Ovechkin. In the playoffs, "Gino" recorded 20 points in 22 games as the Penguins reached the Stanley Cup finals for the first time since 1992, before losing to the Detroit Red Wings.

For the second straight year, Malkin finished as runner-up to Ovechkin in Hart Trophy voting at the end of the 2008–09 season, but he walked away with plenty of hardware of his own. Malkin won the Art Ross Trophy as the NHL's leading scorer in the regular season with 35 goals and 113 points. He followed that with a league-leading 36 points in 24 playoff games and a Conn Smythe Trophy win as playoff MVP, after Pittsburgh turned the tables on the Red Wings to win the Stanley Cup in seven games.

Malkin was the first player to lead the NHL in both regular-season and playoff scoring since current Penguins owner Mario Lemieux did it as a player in 1991–92. Malkin also became the first Russian-born player to win the Conn Smythe Trophy.

With a young core of star players that also included goaltender Marc-Andre Fleury and defenceman Kris Letang, it looked like the Penguins were on their way to becoming a dynasty. But after these consecutive trips to the Stanley Cup finals, injuries became an issue for both Malkin and Crosby. In 2010–11, Malkin was limited to just 43 games. He missed the last two months of the regular season and all of the playoffs after undergoing surgery on his right knee.

After his rehabilitation, Malkin came back strong. In 2011–12, he hit the 50-goal mark for the only time in his career and won his second Art Ross Trophy with 109 points. Malkin was also named the NHL's most valuable player, winning the Hart Trophy for the first time, and won the Lester B. Pearson Trophy as league MVP as chosen by his fellow players.

In the five seasons since hitting that high-water mark, Malkin's personal achievements have taken a back seat to his team play. Though plagued by a variety of ailments, he has continued to be a steady point producer in today's lower-scoring NHL. He is versatile enough to be effective as either a centreman or winger, and on the power play, he is as good as it gets.

The Penguins went six seasons without advancing past the conference finals before a mid-season coaching change in 2015–16 ignited Malkin and the rest of his teammates. Under the guidance of Mike Sullivan, the Penguins used their speed to their advantage and beat the New York Rangers, Washington Capitals, Tampa Bay Lightning, and San Jose Sharks on their way to winning the 2016 Stanley Cup.

Despite the difficulty of being a dominant team in the salary-cap era, there was no Stanley Cup hangover in Pittsburgh. The Penguins hovered near the top of the NHL standings and ultimately finished second overall in 2016–17 before another successful trip to the Stanley Cup finals in the spring of 2017.

Malkin jumped out to an early lead in the playoff scoring race with 11 points in the five games of Pittsburgh's first-round series win over the Columbus Blue Jackets. Going into Game 6 of the Cup finals against the Nashville Predators, he continued to lead the playoff scoring race with 28 points in 24 games, one ahead of his teammate Crosby. The Penguins won that game, 2–0, becoming the first team to repeat since Detroit nearly two decades earlier.

On the international front, Malkin has answered the call for his native Russia whenever he has had the opportunity. In addition to his U18 and World Junior tournaments, he's a seven-time member of Russia's World Championship team and has six medals to show for his efforts: two gold (2012, 2014), two silver (2010, 2015), and two bronze (2005, 2007). He was named most valuable player at the 2012 tournament in Finland, where he led all skaters with 11 goals and 19 points in 10 games.

Malkin has also played in three Olympics (2006, 2010, 2014) and in the 2016 World Cup of Hockey, but he was unable to capture a medal at any of those events. Nevertheless, Malkin has proven his worth in the NHL as a star, a teammate to an even greater star (Crosby), and a team player who has been an integral part of three Stanley Cup wins in Pittsburgh.

To look at Mitch Marner up close is to look at a paradox in the hockey world. Marner could hide behind a straw, probably couldn't do five chin-ups, and couldn't score on a slapshot to save his life.

But, without question, he's also one of the best young players in the NHL today.

What makes him so effective? The new term is "hockey IQ," meaning he has great vision, great patience, and great calm. He is also a sensational passer, so much so that to a fault he'll look to pass first and think shot a distant second.

Marner had an outstanding junior career with the London Knights (2013–16). During these three years, he developed into a top prospect and a team leader. As a rookie, he had but 13 goals and 59 points in 64 games, but in his second season, he scored 44 goals and added 82 assists and finished second in OHL scoring only because Dylan Strome recorded six points on the final day to overtake Marner.

To make his year all the sweeter, Marner was drafted fourth overall by the team he idolized as a kid, the Maple Leafs.

## MITCH MARNER

B. MARKHAM, ONTARIO, MAY 5, 1997
6'0" 170 LBS.
CENTRE/SHOOTS RIGHT
DRAFTED 4TH OVERALL
BY TORONTO IN 2015
NHL DEBUT OCTOBER 12, 2016
@MARNER93

In what proved to be his final year of junior, 2015–16, Marner had a season for the ages. He was named the OHL's MVP (after finishing second in scoring again, this time with 116 points) and led the Knights to victory in the Memorial Cup. He led all players in playoff scoring in the OHL, was named MVP of the Memorial Cup finals, and led the finals in scoring as well.

Marner made the Leafs at training camp in 2016, a historic year for the Leafs. They now had first-overall draft choice from 2016, Auston Matthews, in the lineup, and young William Nylander was also ready for the NHL. This troika formed the core of a young and exciting Leafs team that drew league-wide praise for its skill and brought hope to playoff-starved Leafs fans.

Marner did his part, to be sure. Playing on a line with Tyler Bozak and James van Riemsdyk, Marner scored 19 goals and 61 points in 77 games as a rookie, impressive numbers to be sure — despite being overshadowed by Matthews's tremendous first year.

What was most impressive about Marner was his ability to play at the world's highest level with the same success as in junior. When he handled the puck, he was calm. He drew opponents to him and then made sensational passes to open teammates. He and Matthews developed chemistry and friendship off ice, and their playful natures captured the hearts of Leafs Nation.

Marner might not be big, but the NHL is getting smaller and faster, and he is among the brightest lights of the new game.

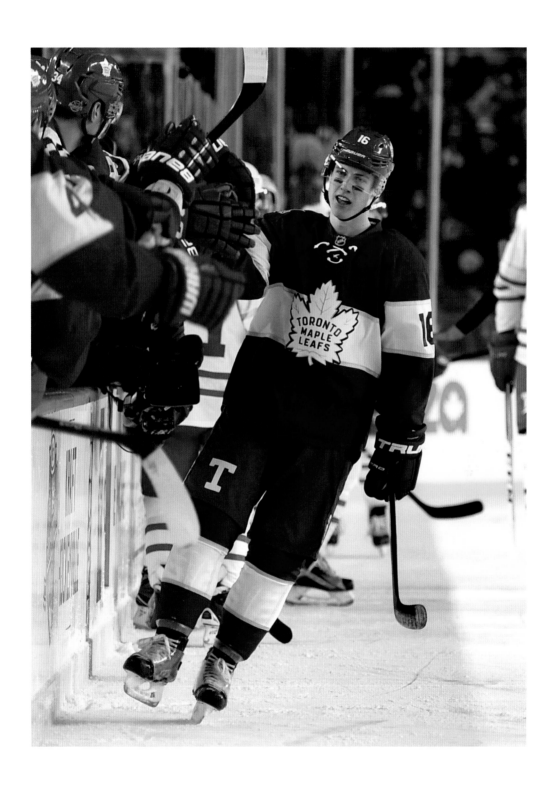

Born in San Ramon, California, and raised in Scottsdale, Arizona, Auston Matthews defied hockey stereotypes as a desert kid who became a first-overall draft pick and is now on track to become one of the best players of his generation.

The list of Matthews's strengths is a long one. He has outstanding size and has shown impressive durability, explosive skating, excellent offensive instincts, and a natural grasp for the defensive elements of the game. After one NHL season, Matthews is well ahead of his expected development curve and is surely only going to get better.

Matthews comes from an athletic family. His great-uncle, Wes Matthews, was a wide receiver with the Miami Dolphins in 1966, and his father, Brian, played baseball in college.

Auston's interest in hockey may never have been piqued if the Winnipeg Jets hadn't relocated to Arizona in 1996. At two years old, Matthews accompanied his father and uncle to a Phoenix Coyotes game, a moment that set the course for his future.

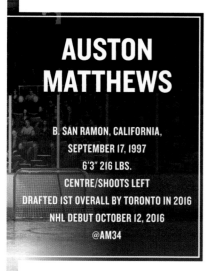

**AUSTON MATTHEWS**

B. SAN RAMON, CALIFORNIA, SEPTEMBER 17, 1997
6'3" 216 LBS.
CENTRE/SHOOTS LEFT
DRAFTED 1ST OVERALL BY TORONTO IN 2016
NHL DEBUT OCTOBER 12, 2016
@AM34

His outstanding hand-eye coordination made him an excellent baseball player, but Matthews preferred the fast pace and continuous action that hockey provided. He first laced up his skates at age five and later signed with the Arizona Bobcats minor hockey program. By the time he reached adolescence, he was skipping baseball practices to spend more time shooting pucks. Hockey had won.

Arizona doesn't have the same minor-hockey infrastructure as northern states like Minnesota or Michigan, but it does boast a long list of one-time NHL players who have settled in the desert after retirement. Many of them stay involved with the game by coaching at the youth level, offering outstanding guidance and support to kids from the region.

In 2012, Matthews was drafted 57th overall by the Everett Silvertips of the WHL, but he elected to join the USA Hockey's National Team Development Program. He moved to Michigan for the 2013–14 season, where he spent time with both the U17 and U18 teams.

Despite missing three months of action after breaking his left femur in his second game with the U17 team, Matthews had a successful season, especially internationally. He had four goals and eight points in six games to win gold with Team USA in January 2014 at the World U17 Hockey Challenge, then added another gold medal in April with seven points in the 2014 U18 World Championship.

In his second season with the NTDP, Matthews exploded to lead his U18 squad with 55 goals and 116 points in 60 games. At 17, he was the youngest player on Team USA at the 2015

World Junior Championship. He then led all players with 15 points and was named most valuable player as the United States captured its second-straight gold medal at the 2015 U18 World Championship in Switzerland.

As he had clearly outgrown his level of competition, Matthews elected to forego the NCAA route that he had initially considered for the 2015–16 season, instead signing on to play professional hockey in a top European men's league, with the ZSC Lions of the Swiss National League A (NLA) in Zurich. Lions coach Marc Crawford was instrumental in bringing Matthews to his team. A former NHL defenceman who had logged 1,151 games as the bench boss of five different NHL teams, Crawford was astonished by Matthews's play at the U18 tournament in Berne and quickly contacted agent Pat Brisson to set the wheels in motion.

Matthews made his pro debut with the Lions on September 18, 2015, one day after his 18th birthday. He foreshadowed his NHL debut one year later by scoring in his first NLA game.

While he waited for his opportunity to be drafted, Matthews lived with his mother, Ema, and older sister, Alexandria, in Zurich. He netted about $400,000 for the season, in which he finished second in team scoring with 24 goals and 46 points in 36 games. Despite missing six games during the season with a back injury, Matthews was given the NLA's Rising Star Award and finished second in MVP voting.

Matthews took time off at mid-season to join Team USA for his third World Junior Championship; this time, he finished fourth in tournament scoring with 11 points, was named to the all-star team, and brought home a bronze medal.

At season's end, he played in the men's World Championship for the first time and didn't look out of place. Another 18-year-old, Patrik Laine of Finland, captured the MVP title, but Matthews wasn't far behind, leading the U.S. team with six goals as the Americans finished fourth in the tournament.

Matthews evened the score with Laine one month later at the 2016 draft. He was chosen first overall, as expected, by the Toronto Maple Leafs while Laine went second, to the Winnipeg Jets.

Before making his NHL debut, Matthews suited up for one more international competition — this time scoring two goals and adding an assist in three games with the high-octane Team North America at the World Cup of Hockey, played in what would soon be his home rink at the Air Canada Centre in Toronto.

On October 12, 2016, Matthews played his first official NHL game, and it was one for the ages. On the road at the Canadian Tire Centre, Matthews scored all four Toronto goals in the Leafs' 5–4 overtime loss to the Ottawa Senators.

The game marked the first time in modern NHL history that a player scored four goals in his league debut. Matthews didn't quite keep up his 328-goal pace for the rest of the season, but he did end the year at the top of the rookie scoring race in both goals (40) and points (69) and earned a nomination for the Calder Trophy as rookie of the year.

Matthews's 40 goals and 69 points both set new records for a Toronto rookie. He also set a new standard for an American-born rookie and tied with Nikita Kucherov for second place overall in the NHL's goal-scoring race behind Sidney Crosby (44).

Showing a flair for the dramatic, eight of Matthews's goals were game-winners, and none was more spectacular than his overtime tally against the Detroit Red Wings in front of 40,148 fans at the outdoor Centennial Classic on January 1, 2017, at BMO Field in Toronto.

Matthews's arrival in Toronto also coincided with a dramatic turnaround in the team's fortunes. A last-place finish and just 69 points in 2015–16 season led to the team's draft lottery win and their first-overall pick of Matthews. In 2016–17, the Leafs improved by 26 points and earned a playoff berth for the first time in four years thanks to a 40-27-15 record.

Never one to shy away from high-pressure situations, Matthews shone again as the young Leafs pushed the Presidents' Trophy–winning Washington Capitals to six games in the first round of the post-season. Every game was decided by a single goal, and five of the six went to overtime. After going scoreless in the first two games of the series, Matthews then scored in each of the four subsequent games, joining fellow Toronto Maple Leafs forward Wendel Clark (1986) as the only teenagers ever to score in four straight playoff games. At season's end, he was the runaway winner of the Calder Trophy, the first Leafs player so honoured since Brit Selby in 1966.

The weight of expectation is heavy when a young Canadian hockey player is compared to all-time greats such as Wayne Gretzky and Sidney Crosby.

In his first two NHL seasons, Connor McDavid of the Edmonton Oilers has proven that he is worthy of those comparisons. No doubt, he'll carve his own place in hockey history when all is said and done.

Born in Richmond Hill, Ontario, McDavid took to hockey at a very early age and immediately excelled. At four years old, he was playing organized hockey in age groups above his own. Coached by his father, Brian, he won four Ontario Minor Hockey Association championships with the York-Simcoe Express in Aurora, Ontario, then moved on to join the Toronto Marlboros of the Greater Toronto Hockey League for his bantam and minor midget years. He was named player of the year in the GTHL in 2011–12 after recording 79 goals and 209 points in 88 games.

After that otherworldly season, McDavid was granted exceptional player status by Hockey Canada, which allowed him to be drafted into the OHL at age 15. He was just the third player to be so named; his predecessors, John Tavares (2005) and Aaron Ekblad (2011), both went on to be first-overall selections in the NHL draft.

Entering major junior, McDavid was chosen first overall by the Erie Otters and quickly showed that he deserved this designation. The Otters had earned the right to the first-overall selection after a dismal 2011–12 season: they finished last in the 20-team OHL with a record of 10-52-3-3.

In McDavid's first season in Erie, the Otters improved to 19-40-4-5. The young centre posted 66 points to finish second in team scoring and earn the Emms Family Award as the OHL's top first-year player.

## CONNOR MCDAVID

**B. RICHMOND HILL, ONTARIO,
JANUARY 13, 1997**

**6'1" 200 LBS.**

**CENTRE/SHOOTS LEFT**

**DRAFTED 1ST OVERALL BY EDMONTON IN 2015**

**NHL DEBUT OCTOBER 8, 2015**

**@CMCDAVID97**

In April 2013, 16-year-old McDavid made his debut in an IIHF tournament at the U18 level. He was named MVP as the tournament's leading scorer with 14 points in seven games, and Canada captured gold for the first time in five years.

During his second season with the Otters, in 2013–14, McDavid improved to 99 points, fourth overall in the OHL and third on his team. He also suited up for Canada's World Junior team, chipping in four points in seven games in a limited role.

The Otters record improved by a whopping 59 points in 2013–14, landing them in second place in the Midwest Division with 106 points and earning a post-season berth for the first time in three years. In the playoffs, McDavid tied for the Otters' team lead with 19 points in 14 games before his team fell to the Guelph Storm in the Western Conference finals.

As dedicated as he is to hockey, McDavid didn't neglect his academics during his time in

junior. He was a two-time winner of the Bobby Smith Trophy, given to the OHL's scholastic player of the year, in 2013–14 and 2014–15.

McDavid's third OHL season was his draft year, and he made the most of it. Now the Otters captain, he increased his goals to 44 and his assists to 76 to finish third in league scoring with 120 points, and he led his team to first place in the Midwest Division.

In the playoffs, he tallied a league-leading 49 points in 20 games, but the Otters fell to the Oshawa Generals in the OHL finals. He was named the OHL's outstanding player in the regular season and playoff MVP and earned CHL player of the year honours. Not surprisingly, he was also named the top draft-eligible prospect. He left the Otters as the most-decorated player in OHL history.

Midway through the 2014–15 season, McDavid served as an alternate captain at his second World Junior Championship. With 11 points in seven games, he tied for the tournament scoring lead and was named to the all-star team. He won a gold medal at the Air Canada Centre in Toronto, less than an hour away from where he grew up.

The Toronto Maple Leafs had finished 27th out of 30 teams in the 2014–15 NHL standings, which gave them a chance of earning a lottery win and the opportunity to draft their hometown prodigy. But the ping-pong balls fell in favour of the Edmonton Oilers. Choosing first overall for the fourth time in just six years, the Oilers brass didn't hesitate to select McDavid and quickly make him the face of their franchise.

Some players could have wilted under the pressure that was heaped on McDavid in Edmonton, but he thrived on it. Immediately displaying his impressive speed, blinding acceleration, and creative moves with the puck, the 18-year-old was named rookie of the month for October 2015, after leading all rookies with 12 points in nine games.

McDavid's maiden tour through the NHL was put on hold on November 3, 2015, however, after he was pushed into the end boards by Brandon Manning of the Philadelphia Flyers while on a short-handed breakaway. The resulting fall led to a broken clavicle, which caused McDavid to miss three months of action.

When he returned to the ice in early February, McDavid picked up where he left off, finishing the year with 11 goals, including four game-winners, to go along with 25 assists in Edmonton's final 32 games of the season. McDavid finished third overall in team scoring as the Oilers improved by eight points in the league standings. He also finished third in Calder Trophy voting, despite missing 37 games. He ranked fourth in rookie scoring, but his 1.07 points per game were third overall in the entire NHL behind Patrick Kane and Jamie Benn.

With plenty of hockey left in him after his fragmented season, McDavid seized the opportunity to join Team Canada at the World Championship for the first time. He scored only one goal in Russia, but it was the tournament winner in Canada's 2–0 gold-medal triumph over Finland.

McDavid returned to Toronto in September, where his speed and his stick-handling skills fit in perfectly on the Under-24 Team North America at the World Cup of Hockey.

Back in Edmonton, the Oilers started the 2016–17 season in their luxurious new arena, Rexall Place, and with an exciting new captain: 19-year-old McDavid. The season proved to be a thrill-a-minute exercise in excitement as the Oilers surged to a 7-1-0 start and McDavid quickly parked himself atop the NHL scoring race — matching his rookie year with five goals and seven assists in the month of October.

This time around, there was no injury to slow him down. Following in the footsteps of Sidney Crosby, McDavid finished atop the NHL scoring race and won the Art Ross Trophy in his second season. With 30 goals and 70 assists, he was the only player to hit the century mark in points in 2016–17. And at 20 years old, he was the third-youngest Art Ross winner in NHL history, behind Crosby and Gretzky.

The Oilers also saw a 33-point improvement in the standings, earning their first playoff berth since 2006. After knocking off the 2016 Stanley Cup finalists San Jose Sharks in six games in their first-round series, they went toe-to-toe with the Anaheim Ducks before falling in seven games. Drawing the toughest checking assignments, McDavid collected five goals and nine points and was a plus-3 in 13 playoff games.

In the summer of 2017, McDavid signed a massive contract extension, an eight-year deal worth a whopping $100 million. He won the Art Ross Trophy, Hart Trophy, and Ted Lindsay Award, and now, new deal in place, he is the league's star attraction.

As a youngster growing up in the Toronto suburb of Brampton, Ontario, Sean Monahan spent his childhood playing sports. Hockey and lacrosse were his passions, and Monahan excelled well enough at Canada's official winter sport to forge what has been a productive, dynamic NHL career.

Monahan starred for the minor midget Mississauga Rebels, posting 13 points in seven games at the 2009–10 OHL Cup en route to claiming MVP honours for the tournament. He caught the eye of the Ottawa 67s and was summarily selected by the major junior team in the first round of the Ontario Hockey League Priority Selection Draft.

The following season, Monahan, then 16, not only collected a respectable 47 points in 65 regular-season games in his first year with Ottawa but also won a gold medal with Ontario at the World U17 Hockey Challenge.

Monahan bumped up his production to 78 points in 2011–12, playing on a talent-laden 67s squad that included future NHLers Tyler Toffoli, Shane Prince, and Cody Ceci. In the post-season, Ottawa advanced to the conference finals before bowing out to Niagara. Monahan registered eight goals and 15 points in 18 playoff games. That summer, he won a gold medal with Team Canada at the annual Under-18 Ivan Hlinka Memorial Cup in the Czech Republic.

**SEAN MONAHAN**

B. BRAMPTON, ONTARIO, OCTOBER 12, 1994
6'3" 195 LBS.
CENTRE/SHOOTS LEFT
DRAFTED 6TH OVERALL
BY CALGARY IN 2013
NHL DEBUT OCTOBER 3, 2013
@MONAHAN20

In his third junior season, 2012–13, Monahan assumed the captaincy with Ottawa and matched his point total from the previous year. By then, he had soared into the upper echelon of the Central Scouting rankings and, sure enough, the Calgary Flames selected him with their first-round pick (6th overall).

Monahan was impressive enough in training camp to avoid being assigned to the 67s for his final junior year; instead, he suited up in a Calgary uniform on October 3, 2013, making his debut for the Flames in Washington. He earned an assist in the outing.

A day later, Monahan netted his first career big-league goal, getting the better of Columbus goalie Sergei Bobrovsky. It was the beginning of a four-game goal streak for the fresh-faced rookie, the last on the day before his 19th birthday.

Altogether, Monahan compiled 22 goals and 34 points in 75 games in his rookie campaign, incurring only four minor penalties all year. He garnered enough attention to finish eighth in the balloting for the Calder Trophy.

Monahan was then invited to play for his country at the 2014 World Championship, and the team looked poised to take home a medal. Canada posted a 5-1-1 record in the round robin but was upset in the quarter-finals versus Finland and eventually finished a disappointing fifth. During the tournament, Monahan posted two assists in eight games.

In 2014–15, Monahan enjoyed a breakout sophomore year that was given an enormous boost with the arrival of fresh-faced Johnny Gaudreau. Coach Bob Hartley assembled a line with Monahan at centre flanked by Gaudreau on the left side and Jiri Hudler on the right wing, and the move paid enormous dividends. The trio became one of the most dangerous, explosive forward units in hockey. By season's end, the top three scorers on the Flames were all members of that line. Hudler, Gaudreau, and Monahan finished with 76, 64, and 62 points, respectively, Monahan recording 31 goals and as many assists.

By taking only 18 penalty minutes in the regular season, Monahan finished fifth in voting for the Lady Byng Trophy. A faceoff specialist showing a keen ability to play at both ends of the rink, Monahan also received several Selke Trophy votes as well. In his first taste of the NHL playoffs in 2015, Monahan notched six points in 11 games.

Even when Hudler's 2015–16 season was curtailed by injury, Monahan and Gaudreau continued to complement each other as the Flames' most dangerous scoring threat. Monahan had a career year with 63 points, but Calgary's season ended in disappointment, out of the playoffs.

On February 23, 2017, in a game against Tampa Bay, Monahan achieved an incredible milestone: he became the youngest player in Flames history to score his 100th career goal (at 22 years, 134 days). By season's end, he had 107 goals in 319 career regular-season games.

Like many young players, Monahan has taken to Twitter to create an alter ego, Boring Sean Monahan (@boringmonahan). But his online persona is in direct contrast to his on-ice playmaking that has continued to dazzle legions of Flames fans.

Despite the Swedish surname and passport, William Nylander has more than a bit of Canadian and American in him. He was born in Calgary while his father, Michael, was playing with the Calgary Flames, and he spent several years in the U.S. as his dad continued his career. But William's heart and culture are Swedish.

He grew up in a hockey environment and had all the benefits one might imagine a hockey-loving kid would have with an NHLer for a dad. The family returned to Sweden when William was 14, and it was there he developed his formidable talents.

Known for his dynamic offensive abilities, he was drafted eighth overall by the Toronto Maple Leafs in 2014, the second-highest European after Leon Draisaitl (third, Edmonton). But the Leafs weren't going to rush him to the big show, and Nylander clearly wasn't ready. Not big to start with, he needed to develop physically and gain more experience playing above junior hockey.

He stared the 2014–15 season back in Sweden, with Modo, and had an excellent World Junior tournament over Christmas. That impressed the Leafs enough that they assigned him to the AHL Marlies to continue his progress. In 37 games with the team, he had 14 goals and 32 points.

Nylander started the 2015–16 season with the Marlies and played his second World Juniors at the end of the year. He was finally called up to the Leafs on Leap Year Day, 2016. A week into his NHL career, he scored his first goal, one that had an amazing bit of trivia attached to it: the goal was assisted by Brooks Laich, who also assisted on Michael Nylander's last goal in the NHL back in 2009.

History might well show that the fall of 2016 was a pivotal one in Leafs' history. As Auston Matthews and Mitch Marner made their NHL debuts, Nylander also made the Leafs full-time, leaving Sweden, the AHL, and words like "prospect" far behind. Often playing on a line with Matthews and Zach Hyman, Nylander scored 22 goals and 61 points in his first full season.

The Leafs made the playoffs but were eliminated in six games. Nylander (and Marner) continued their season at the World Championship. Nylander was a dominant force for Tre Kronor and helped his country beat Marner and Canada 2–1 in the gold-medal game. In all, Nylander had seven goals and as many assists in 10 games and was named tournament MVP.

Nylander is part of an amazing group of young Leafs who, together, seem capable of delivering deep playoff performances to fans. His quick shot and speed with the puck separate him from most NHLers, and he looks to be a superstar for years to come.

## WILLIAM NYLANDER

B. CALGARY, ALBERTA, MAY 1, 1996
6'0" 190 LBS.
CENTRE/SHOOTS RIGHT
DRAFTED 8TH OVERALL
BY TORONTO IN 2014
NHL DEBUT FEBRUARY 29, 2016
@WMNYLANDER

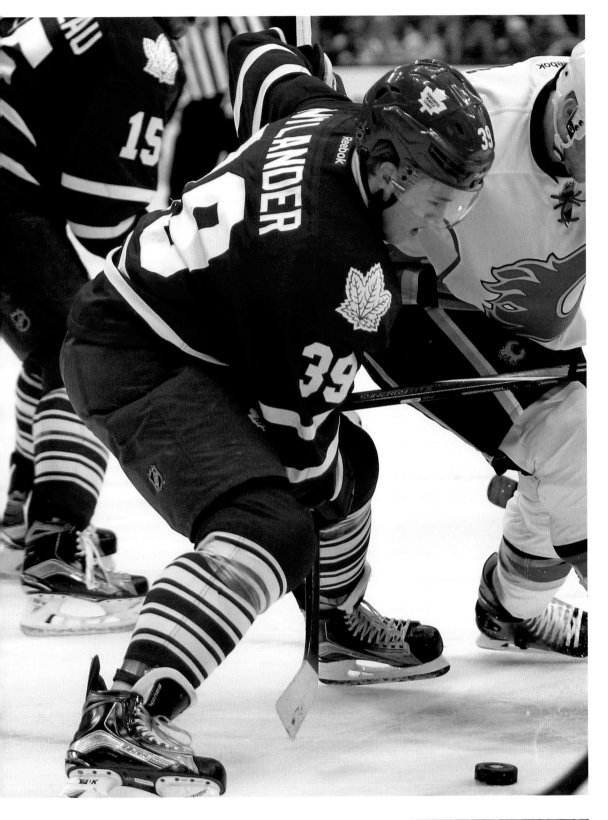

One of the greatest scorers ever to play in the NHL, Alexander Ovechkin has been a goal-scoring machine for the Washington Capitals for the last 12 seasons.

During that time, Ovechkin has won six Rocket Richard Trophies as the league's leading goal-scorer, as well as the Calder Trophy as rookie of the year, three Hart Trophies as league MVP, three Lester B. Pearson/Ted Lindsay Awards as most valuable player selected by the members of the NHLPA, and the Art Ross Trophy as leading scorer.

Missing from his trophy case? An Olympic medal and a Stanley Cup ring.

Ovechkin was born in Moscow, the youngest of three boys. His mother, Tatyana, was a fine athlete — a two-time Olympic gold medallist with the Soviet Union's women's basketball team in 1976 and 1980 — who now runs the Russian national women's basketball program.

Young Alexander was intrigued by hockey at an early age and was encouraged in his love for the sport by his oldest brother, Sergei. Alexander enrolled in his first hockey school at the age of eight but suffered an emotional loss at age 10, when Sergei passed away following a car accident.

## ALEXANDER OVECHKIN

B. MOSCOW, SOVIET UNION (RUSSIA),
SEPTEMBER 17, 1985
6'3" 239 LBS.
LEFT WING/SHOOTS RIGHT
DRAFTED 1ST OVERALL
BY WASHINGTON IN 2004
NHL DEBUT OCTOBER 5, 2005
@OVI8

Passionate and determined, Ovechkin joined Dynamo Moscow of the Russian Superleague in 2001 at age 16. In three seasons leading up to the 2004 draft, he accumulated 23 goals and 19 assists in 114 games.

More importantly, Ovechkin dazzled with Team Russia on international ice. In his first World U18 tournament at age 16 in April 2002, he led all players with 14 goals and 18 points in eight games, helping Russia win a silver medal. He followed up with a bronze medal at the 2003 U18 tournament, scoring nine goals and adding four assists in six games. Ovechkin's scoring prowess and blistering shot were already making the player famous. He set all-time records for goals (23) and points (31) at the U18 tournament.

At 17, Ovechkin took to the ice in the first of three World Junior Championships on his résumé. His six goals in six games tied for tops in the tournament as Russia won gold with a 3–2 win over Canada in Halifax, Nova Scotia. He added five more goals when Russia was eliminated in the quarter-finals in the 2004 tournament, then won a silver medal and was named to the tournament all-star team when he tallied six more goals in 2005.

Ovechkin had been regarded so highly since his breakout performance at the World Juniors in Halifax that Florida Panthers general manager Rick Dudley hatched a plan to try to grab him one year early. Ovechkin's birthday falls just two days after the September 15 draft cutoff date, so Dudley attempted to argue that once leap years were factored in, he was, indeed, old enough

to be considered 18 before the cutoff for the 2003 draft. Since the same terms would apply to all players, Dudley was rebuffed.

Going into his draft year in 2004, Ovechkin was the sure number-one pick — renowned not just for his shot but also for his size, speed, and enthusiasm for the game. Sure enough, on June 26, 2004, in Raleigh, North Carolina, the Capitals chose him with their first pick. He was the second Russian player to be chosen first overall, after Ilya Kovalchuk in 2001.

The 2004–05 NHL lockout meant that Ovechkin had to return to Russia for another season with Dynamo Moscow before his North American career could begin. Before that happened, he got a teaser of NHL competition when the 18-year-old was Russia's youngest player in the 2004 World Cup of Hockey. He suited up for two games, scoring once, before Russia was eliminated by the United States in the quarter-finals.

When Ovechkin finally made his NHL debut with the Capitals in October 2005, it set up a thrilling rivalry with the top pick chosen one year after him, Canadian Sidney Crosby.

The Canada-versus-Russia story was catnip to hockey journalists, and in the first chapter, Ovechkin emerged victorious — dominating the sombre Crosby with his palpable love for the game and outscoring him as well. Both players lived up to their billing by recording more than 100 points in their rookie season, but Ovechkin's 52 goals and 106 points bested the 39 goals and 102 points for Crosby and earned him the top rookie honours.

Between 2007–08 and 2009–10, Ovechkin enjoyed the best run of his NHL career. In 2007–08, he logged his career highs to date of 65 goals and 112 points, setting up a run of two scoring titles, two Hart Trophies, and three straight Pearson Trophies (renamed the Ted Lindsay Award in 2009–10). Ovechkin added another 20 goals over three playoff years but while the Capitals consistently stretched their series to seven games, they won just once in four tries.

That pattern of post-season futility led to a steady string of appearances at the World Championship once Ovechkin's NHL seasons ended. Starting in 2005, while he was still in Russia, he suited up for Team Russia in 10 of 11 years, earning three gold, two silver, and three bronze medals.

Ovechkin has also played in three Olympics but has yet to earn a medal. In 2006, he was named to the all-tournament team and scored the game-winning goal that eliminated the defending champions, Canada, from competition. Coming into the 2010 Games as one of the world's best players, he disappointed by scoring only four points in four games before Russia was eliminated in the quarter-finals.

Expectations in host nation Russia were sky high as Ovechkin led his team into Sochi in 2014, but once again the Russian team failed to gel. Ovechkin had two points in five games as Russia bowed out early, this time at the quarter-finals stage.

Back in the NHL, Ovechkin struggled to match his early career successes or to break through with a career-defining playoff performance. He was named Washington's captain at the beginning of the 2009–10 season, after his fourth 50-goal year, but he and his team were unable to maintain his early high standard as he moved into his late 20s, when his career should have been at its peak.

After returning to Moscow to play with Dynamo during the 2012–13 NHL lockout, Ovechkin came back to North America recharged, winning his first Rocket Richard Trophy in four years by scoring 32 goals in 48 games. He went on to be Rocket Richard champion for the next three seasons — each time as the only player in the NHL to break the 50-goal plateau.

In November 2015, Ovechkin scored his 484th goal to pass Sergei Fedorov as the Russian-born player with the most NHL goals. Fedorov needed 1,248 games to set his standard; Ovechkin matched him in only 777 games.

Less than two months later, Ovechkin became the fifth-fastest player in NHL history to score 500 goals, notching a power-play marker against the Ottawa Senators on January 10, 2016. At age 31, he ranks 26th among the league's all-time goal scorers with 558, and his career average of .606 goals per game puts him sixth all-time and fourth among players born after 1900 — ahead of scoring greats like Wayne Gretzky, Brett Hull, and Phil Esposito and behind only Mike Bossy, Mario Lemieux, and Pavel Bure.

But for all his scoring genius, the lack of a Stanley Cup might one day come back to hurt his reputation. Time is running out, and he wouldn't be the first great player not to win one, but those who have followed his career know how important he feels it is to his legacy.

During the period of time in which goaltender Carey Price has been the cornerstone of the Montreal Canadiens, the Habs have struggled to find the back of the net. However, their most consistent sniper and the backbone of their offence has undoubtedly been Max Pacioretty.

As a teenager, Pacioretty starred for Taft School in his home state, Connecticut, before suiting up for the Sioux City Musketeers of the USHL. He caught the eye of the Canadiens scouts and was scooped up by Montreal in the first round of the 2007 NHL Entry Draft.

Pacioretty went on to play one season for the University of Michigan Wolverines and spent his Christmas break representing the United States at the 2008 World Junior Championship. He returned to the Wolverines and finished the year with an impressive 15 goals and 39 points in 37 games.

The following year, Pacioretty was assigned to the Hamilton Bulldogs of the American Hockey League. He received the long-awaited call from the Habs to make his NHL debut on January 2, 2009. Pacioretty wasted no time in netting his first big-league goal, firing the puck past New Jersey's Scott Clemmensen in a 4–1 Montreal loss.

## MAX PACIORETTY

B. NEW CANAAN, CONNECTICUT,
NOVEMBER 20, 1988
6'2" 215 LBS.
LEFT WING/SHOOTS RIGHT
DRAFTED 22ND OVERALL
BY MONTREAL IN 2007
NHL DEBUT JANUARY 2, 2009
@PATCHES67

In March, he was returned to Hamilton for the remainder of the year, but by October, he had played himself into the Montreal lineup to start the 2009–10 season. By late January, however, Pacioretty had just three goals in 52 games and was returned to the minors in the hopes that he would regain his confidence.

The additional time spent with the Bulldogs benefited Pacioretty enormously. He was promoted to the Habs in December 2010 and promptly fired off a respectable 24 points in 37 games.

Then disaster struck. On March 8, 2011, the Boston Bruins paid a visit to Montreal's Bell Centre. In the dying seconds of the second period, Pacioretty was crushed hard by Boston Bruins defenceman Zdeno Chara into a stanchion located on the edge of an area of Plexiglas that separated the players' benches. The controversial hit resulted in a concussion and broken vertebrae, ending Pacioretty's season.

Pacioretty recovered from his injuries in time for the start of the 2011–12 season. The trio of Pacioretty, David Desharnais, and Erik Cole became Montreal's top forward line. In a breakout year that included his first NHL hat trick, Pacioretty scored 33 goals in 79 games while leading his team in scoring with 65 points.

Notably, Pacioretty became the first American-born player to score 30 goals in a season in a Canadiens uniform. The campaign marked the first of six consecutive years that Pacioretty

led the Canadiens in scoring. His remarkable comeback year was duly recognized when he was awarded the Bill Masterton Trophy for perseverance, sportsmanship, and dedication to hockey.

At the 2012 World Championship, Pacioretty collected an impressive two goals and 10 assists in eight games for the United States. By 2013–14, Pacioretty's ability to fire the puck with laser-like precision was wreaking havoc on opposing goalies. In February, he received an invitation to play for Team USA on the world's biggest stage, the Olympics in Sochi. Alas, he didn't come home with a medal. Pacioretty registered only one assist in five games, and the Americans were blanked by Finland, 5–0, in the bronze-medal game.

More positively, Pacioretty finished the NHL's 2013–14 season with a career-high 39 goals and also led the league with 11 game-winners. The Habs went on an impressive playoff run to the conference finals, eventually falling to the New York Rangers. Pacioretty collected 11 points in 17 post-season games.

Although the Habs still lacked a point-per-game player, Pacioretty continued not only to be the sparkplug on Montreal's forward unit but also a solid two-way skater in the tradition of Bob Gainey. In 2014–15, Pacioretty posted his third consecutive season of 30 or more goals (37) and finished fifth in voting for the Selke Trophy. It was also a season in which he was named one of four co-captains for the Habs.

The next year, Pacioretty assumed the captaincy on a full-time basis. The following season, 2016–17, was highlighted by two events: a call to play for Team USA at the World Cup of Hockey, and a career-high four-goal game in a rout of Colorado on December 10, 2016.

The man they call "Patches" has been a mainstay for two teams that wear the same colours: the *bleu, blanc, et rouge* of the Habs and the red, white, and blue of the United States. His dual career has made him one of the U.S.'s best players of the 2010s.

Artemi Panarin of the Columbus Blue Jackets has something in common with Joe Mullen, Martin St. Louis, and Tyler Johnson: all of them are small, nifty forwards who were never drafted, but that didn't stop them from becoming NHL stars. For Panarin, getting some extra time to hone his skills in his native Russia has paid off handsomely.

He grew up near Chelyabinsk, an industrial city in the Ural Mountains that produced Soviet star Sergei Makarov, who was named to the IIHF Centennial All-Star Team in 2008. Like Makarov, Panarin gained attention for his electrifying stickhandling and skating. Unsurprisingly, the teenager also idolized Detroit's Pavel Datsyuk. Panarin played most of his first five KHL seasons with Vityaz in Chekhov, and there were some rough times. Although the club's GM was former NHLer Alexei Zhamnov, a consummate finesse player, Vityaz was known for playing "goon hockey." Vityaz never made the KHL playoffs during Panarin's tenure.

However, the diminutive left wing starred in Russia's 5–3 comeback win over Canada in the 2011 World Junior Championship gold-medal game. Playing on a line with fellow Chelyabinsk product Evgeni Kuznetsov, Panarin scored two lovely third-period goals, including the game-winner, as coach Valeri Bragin's team rallied from a 3–0 deficit to stun the pro-Canada crowd in Buffalo.

## ARTEMI PANARIN

B. KORKINO, SOVIET UNION (RUSSIA),
OCTOBER 30, 1991
5'11" 170 LBS.
LEFT WING/SHOOTS RIGHT
UNDRAFTED
NHL DEBUT OCTOBER 7, 2015
@9ARTEMI

His KHL fortunes truly improved when he was traded to SKA St. Petersburg in 2013. With the rich club in Russia's second-largest city, Panarin saw more ice time and tied for the team lead in scoring with veteran sniper Ilya Kovalchuk (40 points) in 2013–14. When Vyacheslav Bykov, who had coached Russia to back-to-back World Championship gold medals in 2008 and 2009, took over behind SKA's bench, things got even better for Panarin.

His line, with centre Vadim Shipachyov and right wing Evgeni Dadonov, became a dominant force. Panarin set career highs with 26 goals and 62 points, finishing fourth in league scoring. He added another 20 playoff points as SKA defeated Ak Bars Kazan in the finals to win its first ever Gagarin Cup.

Just like that, Panarin was a hot free-agent commodity for NHL teams. Wisely, he opted to sign with the perennial contender Chicago Blackhawks, inking a two-year entry deal on April 29, 2015. However, he wasn't part of the Hawks' third Cup run during the era of Jonathan Toews and Patrick Kane that spring. He was already committed to making his World Championship debut in the Czech Republic. Playing with his usual SKA linemates, Panarin racked up 10 points as Russia settled for silver after a 6–1 final loss to the Sidney Crosby–led Canadians.

Panarin put that disappointment behind him with a spectacular rookie season for Chicago. Teammates nicknamed him the "Bread Man," since his surname sounds like the Panera Bread

restaurant chain, and he cooked up magical chemistry with Kane. Both players thought of the game the same way and made defenders look foolish with their puck-moving abilities.

Teamed with centre Artem Anisimov, Panarin easily won the rookie scoring race with 30 goals and 77 points. Kane, who captured the Art Ross Trophy with 106 points and the Hart Trophy as NHL MVP, was quick to acknowledge that Panarin had been integral to his success.

Chicago's reign as Cup champs ended with a seven-game, first-round loss to the St. Louis Blues. However, Panarin performed creditably, posting two points in both Game 5 and 6 with the Hawks facing elimination. Afterwards, he suited up in Moscow at the 2016 World Championship and dazzled the home crowds with 15 points en route to a bronze medal.

There was some controversy when the 24-year-old Russian earned the Calder Memorial Trophy as the league's top rookie. Some felt that fellow finalist Connor McDavid had been more impressive at age 19, but the Edmonton Oilers wunderkind had played only 45 games due to injury. McDavid got 25 first-place votes, and the other finalist, defenceman Shayne Gostisbehere of the Philadelphia Flyers, got 33 — but they were both outdistanced by Panarin, with 88.

In some respects, Panarin's 2016–17 campaign mirrored the season before. He wound up with 31 goals and 74 points. Once again, the season ended with a first-round disappointment, as the Hawks were swept by the eventual Stanley Cup finalists Nashville Predators. But Panarin showed his boundless potential by leading the World Championship with 17 points in nine games, and Russia won bronze again in Germany. Clearly, the best is still to come for this kid from Korkino.

Creative, daring, and electrifying, David Pastrnak is a special talent whose playmaking has captivated Bruins fans.

Indeed, Pastrnak was a prodigy playing in his native Czech Republic. As a 16-year-old in the 2011–12 season, he split his time between AZ Havirov — a Division 3 men's league team — and HC Ocelari Trinec in the U18 division. With the latter team, he collected a remarkable 33 goals and 47 points in just 31 games.

During the Christmas holidays, Pastrnak represented his country — in his first of many international appearances — at the World Hockey Challenge in Windsor, Ontario. Pastrnak had an assist in five games in the showcase of the world's best Under-17 players.

The following year, he joined Sodertalje SK in Sweden. Although Pastrnak was briefly taking up residence in a different nation, his native land was never far from his heart. The player made his first of two consecutive appearances for the Czech Republic at the 2013 U18 World Championship. The Czechs were bounced 6–0 in the quarter-finals by Canada, and Pastrnak wound up with just two points in five games.

By season's end, Pastrnak, still a year away from NHL draft eligibility, was being heavily scouted, and not just in North America. He was a first-round pick of Severstal in the 2013 Kontinental Hockey League draft, although the selection, like so many in the KHL, never came to fruition.

The 2013–14 season was productive for the up-and-coming Pastrnak. He won both a silver medal with the Czechs at the U18 Worlds and a bronze at the Ivan Hlinka Memorial Cup. Registering 29 points in 36 games for Sodertalje's U20 team, Pastrnak also showed a bit of a mean streak as he racked up 67 penalty minutes.

## DAVID PASTRNAK

B. HAVIROV, CZECH REPUBLIC, MAY 25, 1996
6'0" 181 LBS.
RIGHT WING/SHOOTS RIGHT
DRAFTED 25TH OVERALL BY BOSTON IN 2014
NHL DEBUT NOVEMBER 24, 2014
@PASTRNAK96

In June, the 6'0" right winger was chosen by Boston with the Bruins' first-round pick at the 2014 NHL Entry Draft. He was assigned to the team's AHL affiliate in Providence to start the year and was named the league's rookie of the month for October.

The big-league Bruins took notice and recalled Pastrnak. He made his NHL debut on November 24 versus Pittsburgh. The 18-year-old had just under eight minutes of ice time, but not even an overtime winner by Evgeni Malkin could dampen the spirits of the rookie playing his first-ever NHL game.

Pastrnak remained with Boston for six games before being returned to Providence. At the end of 2014, he skated for the first time at the World Junior Championship, collecting three points in five games for the sixth-place Czechs, while also being named one of the top three players for his team.

In the new year, Pastrnak played just one game for Providence before once again being recalled to Boston, where he remained for the rest of the season. Pastrnak's first NHL campaign was respectable. The player amassed 10 goals and 27 points in 46 games. However, he was losing battles along the boards and getting knocked off the puck too easily.

The youngster vowed to develop his speed and strength, and his off-season efforts paid huge dividends. Various injuries limited Pastrnak's 2015–16 season to just 51 games, but the Bruins prospect managed to score 15 goals. He also earned an invitation to play in his second straight World Junior Championship. Pastrnak notched an overtime winner against Denmark in the preliminary round to highlight his tournament.

The next season, 2016–17, was a breakout year for Pastrnak. His season started early when he was named to the Czech Republic roster for the World Cup of Hockey. In October, Bruins coach Claude Julien gave his young protégé the ultimate vote of confidence and moved him to the top line, flanking the right wing alongside Patrice Bergeron and Brad Marchand.

The fiery Pastrnak capitalized on this opportunity. No longer an intimidated, high-risk player, he mystified his opponents with a lethal blend of speed and stickhandling. In a game against Nashville, Pastrnak foiled defender Matt Irwin with a pirouette move that was dazzling enough to go viral on YouTube, even though he didn't score on the play.

Pastrnak recorded seven multi-goal games on the year — one of which occurred on opening night — and finished the year with 34 goals and 70 points in 35 games, second only to Marchand in Bruins scoring.

Despite a shaky beginning to his NHL career, Pastrnak has since evolved into one of the game's most dangerous snipers, and, at 21, his best days are surely still ahead.

In 1993, Alexandre Daigle, the number-one overall draft pick of the Ottawa Senators, famously said, "No one remembers number two." However, that year's second pick, Chris Pronger, went on to a Hall of Fame career, and Sam Reinhart hopes to follow a similar pattern.

Reinhart has the bloodline for hockey excellence. His father, Paul, was among the NHL's most talented defencemen in the 1980s, scoring 560 points in 648 career games, mostly with the Calgary Flames. Paul wrapped up his career with two seasons in Vancouver and settled there, pursuing a career in finance and investing. Sam is the youngest and most gifted of three brothers. The oldest, Max, is a former Calgary prospect, while Griffin, who captained the Edmonton Oil Kings to the 2014 Memorial Cup, has battled to establish himself as an NHL blueliner with the New York Islanders and Edmonton Oilers.

While Sam Reinhart is noted for his on-ice composure today, he sometimes got rowdy when he was growing up. He got in a wrestling match at home with Griffin that resulted in a baseboard heater setting a futon on fire, and the family had to live at Vancouver's Pan Pacific Hotel for two weeks while home repairs were completed. However, while playing for local teams like the bantam Hollyburn Huskies and the major midget Vancouver Northwest Giants, Reinhart built a reputation as a smart two-way centre, similar to Ron Francis or Nicklas Backstrom. During off-seasons, he maximized his athleticism by playing tennis, lacrosse, and soccer.

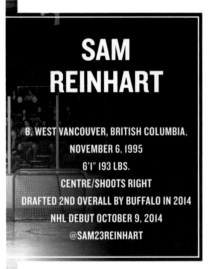

**SAM REINHART**

B. WEST VANCOUVER, BRITISH COLUMBIA,
NOVEMBER 6, 1995
6'1" 193 LBS.
CENTRE/SHOOTS RIGHT
DRAFTED 2ND OVERALL BY BUFFALO IN 2014
NHL DEBUT OCTOBER 9, 2014
@SAM23REINHART

When he graduated to the WHL's Kootenay Ice, Reinhart gained more responsibility each season with the Cranbrook, British Columbia, franchise. His first taste of WHL action was in 2010–11, and the 15-year-old potted the winner against the Oil Kings in his debut. Max was his Kootenay teammate, and Griffin was on the Oil Kings, marking the first time all three brothers played in the same game. Sam also saw limited action as the Ice won the WHL title and participated in the Memorial Cup.

The following season, Reinhart earned 62 points in 67 games at age 16, earning WHL rookie of the year honours. Named an assistant captain in 2012–13, he went on to lead the Ice with 85 points. And as captain in 2013–14, Reinhart exploded for 105 points. He showcased his skills at the annual Top Prospects Game in Calgary, captaining Don Cherry's squad versus Bobby Orr's and chipping in a goal and an assist in a 4–3 loss. Even though the Medicine Hat Tigers eliminated the Ice in the second round of the playoffs, Reinhart excelled with 23 points in 13 games.

Meanwhile, the heady pivot was also making his mark internationally. He got valuable experience in a Team Canada sweater, earning a bronze medal at the IIHF U18 World Championships

in 2012 and a gold medal in 2013. He enjoyed making his World Junior debut alongside Griffin in 2014 in Malmo, Sweden, but Canada lost 2–1 to Russia in the bronze-medal game.

The year 2015, however, was a different story. Reinhart made the NHL to start the year but Buffalo sent him back to junior after nine games. He seized the opportunity to participate in his second World Juniors. Playing in front of Canadian fans in Montreal and Toronto, Reinhart emerged as an all-star and a leader. His line with Max Domi and Anthony Duclair was the tournament's most dangerous, and he topped the scoring parade with five goals and 11 points. In a thrilling 5–4 gold-medal victory over archrival Russia at the Air Canada Centre, Reinhart potted the game winner.

When Reinhart stuck with the Sabres in 2015–16, it seemed poetically appropriate that he wear his father Paul's old number 23, and he also scored 23 goals as an NHL rookie. Despite the franchise's struggles, his season highlight was surely his first hat trick in a 4–2 win over Winnipeg in January.

Buffalo missed the post-season for the seventh straight year in 2016–17, and Reinhart's development stalled. He had 47 points and, after arriving late for the team's morning stretch, was benched for the entirety of a late-season 3–1 loss to Columbus. Still, Reinhart — along with prodigies including Jack Eichel and Rasmus Ristolainen — is too smart and skilled not to become a difference-maker for Buffalo.

One of the core players on a young and promising Maple Leafs team, Morgan Rielly is one of the "veterans" at age 23. Like Wendel Clark three decades earlier, Rielly played pre–major junior hockey at Notre Dame in Wilcox, Saskatchewan, the school made famous by Athol "Pere" Murray.

When he was junior eligible, Rielly played with Moose Jaw for three years (2010–13). He earned a reputation as a big and strong but mobile defenceman. Although he had a great rookie season, his second year was badly damaged by a serious knee injury. The Leafs, however, were not dissuaded and drafted him a lofty fifth overall in 2012, confident he would recover fully and develop into a stud on the blue line.

Rielly, indeed, had an excellent third year with the Warriors in 2012–13, scoring 12 goals and 54 points in 60 games. He started the year helping Canada win gold at the Ivan Hlinka Memorial Cup, and midway through the season he also played at the World Junior Championship in Ufa, Russia. At season's end, he joined the AHL Marlies to get in some pro hockey for the first time.

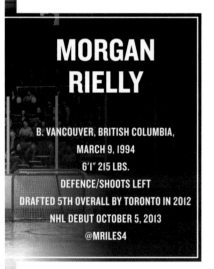

**MORGAN RIELLY**

B. VANCOUVER, BRITISH COLUMBIA,
MARCH 9, 1994
6'1" 215 LBS.
DEFENCE/SHOOTS LEFT
DRAFTED 5TH OVERALL BY TORONTO IN 2012
NHL DEBUT OCTOBER 5, 2013
@MRILES4

The Leafs were in need of defence, and Rielly had an excellent training camp in September 2013, so he made the team at age 19. As a rookie, he managed just two goals but was a respectable minus-13 on a weak team, and his 17:38 of ice time was impressive. At the end of the year, the Leafs missed the playoffs, but Rielly's play impressed Hockey Canada enough that he was invited to play at the World Championship in Minsk, Belarus.

The next year, Rielly improved his offence to eight goals and 29 points and averaged more than 20 minutes of playing time per game. In the summer of 2015, the Leafs hired Mike Babcock as coach, and "Babs" relied heavily on Rielly during what was an otherwise painful year. Rielly averaged more than 23 minutes of ice time, among the top defencemen in the league, but the Leafs finished dead last in the standings.

Rielly again answered the bell to play at the World Championship and was a star on coach Bill Peters's blue line as Canada skated to an impressive gold medal. That fall, Rielly was named to Team North America for the World Cup in Toronto. When he started the NHL season, he was wearing an "A" on his sweater for the Maple Leafs.

At only 23, Rielly already has four years of NHL play under his belt and is one of the leaders on a team expected to compete for the Stanley Cup in the foreseeable future.

Some of Finland's greatest players have worn the sweater of Turku's TPS, notably Saku Koivu, Jere Lehtinen, and Miikka Kiprusoff. Another TPS alumnus, Rasmus Ristolainen of the Buffalo Sabres, has all the tools to forge a long, award-laden career of his own.

In 2010–11, the big-bodied blueliner made his debut in the top Finnish league at age 16. A workout fanatic who grew up idolizing Shea Weber, the owner of the NHL's hardest slap shot, Ristolainen improved by leaps and bounds over the next two seasons with TPS.

During the lockout campaign of 2012–13, his NHL-experienced teammates included Mikko Koivu, Lauri Korpikoski, and Kevin Shattenkirk. At the 2013 NHL draft, Ristolainen became the highest-drafted Finn in Sabres history. He was taken after Edmonton chose Darnell Nurse (seventh) and before Vancouver picked Bo Horvat (ninth).

Few defencemen have the size, strength, and savvy to play in the NHL at age 18, but Ristolainen was up to the challenge. He wound up splitting 2013–14 between the NHL and the AHL, logging 34 games with both the Sabres and the Rochester Americans. GM Tim Murray was happy to burn the first year of Ristolainen's contract in the name of patiently developing the young talent.

## RASMUS RISTOLAINEN

B. TURKU, FINLAND, OCTOBER 27, 1994
6'4" 203 LBS.
DEFENCE/SHOOTS RIGHT
DRAFTED 8TH OVERALL BY BUFFALO IN 2013
NHL DEBUT OCTOBER 2, 2013
@RASMRIST55

Ristolainen had two goals and two assists as an NHL rookie. The always-memorable first goal came on a wrister that beat Jacob Markstrom of the Florida Panthers in a 3–1 road win on October 25, 2013. Bizarrely, Sabres teammate Cody McCormick got into a fight with Panthers defenceman Erik Gudbranson after he went to retrieve the puck as a souvenir for Ristolainen.

The season was a struggle for the Sabres, who missed the playoffs for the third straight time. But Ristolainen will always remember 2014 as a triumphant year. He was loaned to Finland to play in his third-straight World Juniors, and he made the most of it, scoring the spectacular 3–2 overtime winner in the finals against host Sweden in Malmo. The assistant captain motored down the right side, cut to the net, and put a backhander under prone goalie Oscar Dansk. Ristolainen was named the tournament's best defenceman. Two of his teammates, overall points leader Teuvo Teravainen and goalie Juuse Saros, joined him on the tournament all-star team. It was only the third time in history that Finland had won the IIHF's annual U20 showcase.

That experience gave Ristolainen much-needed confidence as he became a full-time NHLer in 2014–15. He had to be mentally tough because there were plenty of ups and downs. Scoring eight goals and 12 assists in 78 games was a nice accomplishment for the teen. Often paired with

another young defenceman, Russia's Nikita Zadorov, against high-calibre forwards, Ristolainen's plus-minus took a hit: he finished a lowly minus-32.

Undeterred, Ristolainen continued to improve in 2015–16. He played a full 82 games for the first time in his NHL career and more than doubled his single-season high in points (41). On December 10, 2015, he scored a hat trick against the Calgary Flames, becoming the first Sabres defenceman to accomplish that feat since Phil Housley in 1988.

While he'd passed up previous opportunities to represent Finland at the World Champion-ship, Ristolainen accepted an invitation to play at the 2016 World Cup of Hockey in Toronto. Unfortunately, the Lions didn't unite in glory, finishing a distant eighth in the eight-team event. Ristolainen went pointless in three games but dressing alongside the likes of Pittsburgh's Olli Maatta and Anaheim's Sami Vatanen was a tribute to his ability.

With the Sabres missing the playoffs yet again in 2016–17, Ristolainen had to look for posi-tives wherever possible. To start the season, Buffalo handed him a six-year, $32.4-million contract, and he responded with a career-high 45 points. In his first career shootout attempt, he scored a lovely one-handed goal versus Jonathan Bernier in a 2–1 win over Anaheim on March 17. Yet later that month, he was suspended for three games for a late hit on Pittsburgh's Jake Guentzel. It was a learning experience for Ristolainen.

If this Finnish workhorse blossoms into a Norris Trophy candidate, it'll be because of his relentless drive to improve. "Everything I do in life, I want to be the best," Ristolainen told the *Buffalo News*. "Why would you do it if you don't want to be the best? I want to always be the best. I want to win."

Size. Speed. Sweet stickhandling skills. Mark Scheifele of the Winnipeg Jets is the total package as an NHL centre, and he still has untapped potential.

In the 2016–17 season, Scheifele finished seventh in NHL scoring with 82 points, another giant step forward for a player whose career has been defined by continuous improvement.

He now looks and plays like a prototypical first-liner, but Scheifele's path to NHL stardom was long and winding. The Kitchener, Ontario, native started out in Junior B with his hometown Kitchener Dutchmen before being chosen in the seventh round of the 2009 OHL junior draft by the Saginaw Spirit. In 2009–10, he posted 18 goals and 37 assists to lead the team in assists and points. At mid-season, he committed to Cornell University for the following year.

In September 2010, the Barrie Colts acquired his rights from the Spirit for overage goaltender Mavric Parks. Scheifele formed an immediate and powerful bond with Barrie's rookie head coach and Winnipeg Jets legend Dale Hawerchuk. Knowing that he could play a key role on a young Colts team, Scheifele elected to forego a career at Cornell to play in the OHL.

**MARK SCHEIFELE**

B. KITCHENER, ONTARIO, MARCH 15, 1993
6'3" 207 LBS.
CENTRE/SHOOTS RIGHT
DRAFTED 7TH OVERALL BY WINNIPEG IN 2011
NHL DEBUT OCTOBER 9, 2011
@MARKSCHEIFELE55

Scheifele made the 2010–11 Colts and finished second in team scoring with 22 goals and 53 assists. He finished fourth among OHL rookies and was named to the second OHL all-rookie team. But one year after challenging the Windsor Spitfires for the OHL championship, a young Colts team in transition finished last in the Central Division and failed to qualify for the playoffs.

Though the Colts were struggling, the buzz grew around Scheifele as the season advanced. In the 2011 mid-season draft rankings, the NHL's Central Scouting ranked him 21st among North American skaters. He put together a strong performance at April's U18 World Championship in Germany, where he tallied eight points in seven games. He was named one of the top players on a fourth-place Canadian team and moved up to 16th in the final Central Scouting rankings.

Going into the draft, Scheifele had clearly made a positive impression on Kevin Cheveldayoff, the new general manager of the resurrected Winnipeg Jets. The Atlanta Thrashers' move to Winnipeg had been finalized less than a month before the draft. The team didn't have a logo or a jersey and had just been officially re-christened the Jets when Cheveldayoff made his way to the stage to make the franchise's first-ever pick.

Cheveldayoff had been on the job less than three weeks as he took the podium at Xcel Energy Center in Minneapolis, just 450 miles from Winnipeg. For his first major move, he defied the popular wisdom of the moment by selecting Scheifele with the seventh-overall pick. When

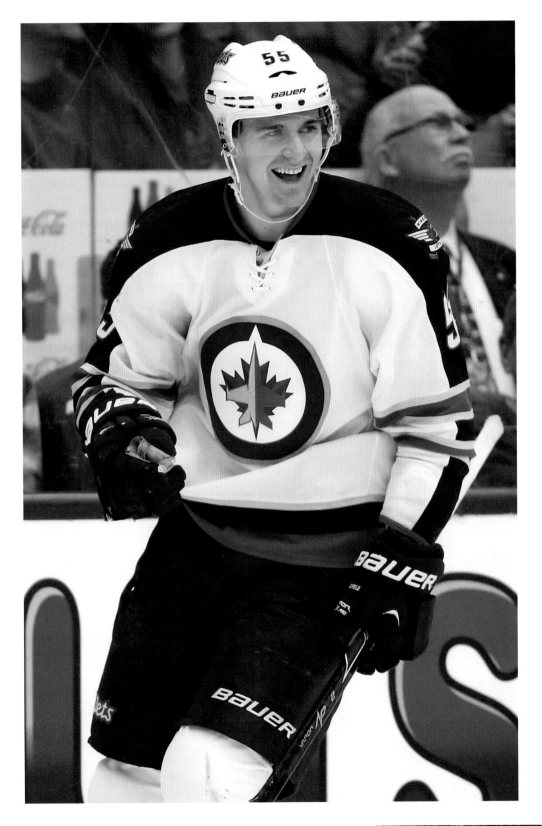

Scheifele's name was called, the teenager was handed a generic black jersey with an NHL logo, which he wore for all his draft photos.

Scheifele wore the new Jets jersey for the first time on October 9, 2011, making his pro debut as the Jets returned to Winnipeg after a 15-year absence.

After scoring one goal in seven NHL games, Scheifele was returned to the Colts, where he posted impressive statistics (23-40-63 in 47 games) for the rest of the 2011–12 season. He finished fourth in team scoring as the Colts moved up to second place in their division and reached the second round of the playoffs.

Once his junior season was over, Scheifele was assigned to the Jets' AHL affiliate, the St. John's IceCaps, where he recorded one assist in 10 playoff games.

Midway through the 2011–12 season, Scheifele was also part of Canada's bronze medal–winning World Junior Championship team at the 2012 tournament co-hosted by Edmonton and Calgary.

Listed at 6'2" and 182 pounds in his final draft ranking, Scheifele worked hard to become NHL-ready by adding size and strength and improving his skills. By the 2012 World Juniors, he tipped the Toledos at 192 pounds.

He played at the same weight when he recorded five goals and eight points in six games at his second World Juniors in Ufa, Russia, in 2013. Scheifele was one of Canada's top players, although the team fell to Russia in the bronze-medal game.

The 2012–13 NHL lockout guaranteed that Scheifele would once again start the season in Barrie. When the labour dispute was settled, he logged four games with the Jets over the course of a month before being returned to the OHL again, his career seemingly stalled.

Scheifele put up 39 goals and 79 points in 45 games in his final junior season, then led the playoffs with 41 points in 21 games, including two five-point games in the OHL finals against the London Knights. But an injury left Scheifele unable to play in the seventh and deciding game of the series, which the Knights ultimately won with a last-second goal.

In 2013–14, Scheifele was listed at 200 pounds as he graduated to the NHL full time. In his rookie season, he scored 13 goals and 34 points in 63 games, but he missed the end of the season after suffering a sprained medial collateral ligament just after the Olympic break, in March. The injury put an end to any chance for Scheifele to compete for the Calder Trophy as the NHL's rookie of the year.

He healed in time to join Team Canada for the 2014 World Championship in Minsk, Belarus, where he picked up four points despite playing limited minutes. Canada fell to Finland in the quarter-finals.

Back in Winnipeg, Scheifele improved his offence in 2014–15 to 15 goals and 49 points and tallied his first career playoff point, an assist, as the Jets reached the post-season for the first time since their return to Winnipeg.

By his third full NHL season, Scheifele was carrying 207 pounds on his 6'3" frame and using his commitment and love for the game to fuel a training regimen that was yielding impressive results. In 2015–16, he moved up to second in Jets scoring with 29 goals and 61 points, breaking the 20-goal plateau with his first career hat trick on March 5, 2016, against the Montreal Canadiens.

When the Jets missed the playoffs, Scheifele once again joined Team Canada. He recorded nine points in nine games as the Canadians captured gold at the 2016 World Championship in Russia.

Coming off his international win, Scheifele followed up with two more milestones during the off-season. In July, he signed an eight-year contract extension with the Jets, with an average annual salary of $6.125 million per season, and in August, he was named one of Winnipeg's alternate captains for the upcoming season.

Off ice, Scheifele trained with Hall of Famer and noted playmaker Adam Oates to further develop his game. His hard work paid off when he hit the ice for the 2016–17 season, starting at the World Cup of Hockey.

Shifted to the wing, Scheifele skated with Connor McDavid and Auston Matthews on the top line of the Under-24 Team North America, which pulled fans out of their seats with its thrilling, high-octane style of play.

That set the stage for another career-best year in Winnipeg, where Scheifele's 82 points were the most for any player since the Jets returned to Winnipeg in 2011.

As part of an 18-point month, Scheifele was named the NHL's second star for the week ending November 13, matching a career high with four points against the Dallas Stars and scoring the shootout winner against Los Angeles.

At season's end, Scheifele returned for his third tour of duty at the World Championship, where Team Canada earned the silver medal after a shootout loss to Sweden in the championship game. He shone on the international ice and proved to a new audience in Paris and Cologne what fans in Winnipeg have known for a while — this guy is good.

Quick-witted and always up for a good time, Tyler Seguin brings fun to the ice, making spectacular plays thanks to his blistering speed and powerful, accurate shot.

Seguin made the NHL as an 18-year-old after being drafted second overall by Boston in 2010. He won the Stanley Cup with the Bruins in his rookie year and made a second trip to the finals in 2012–13. He also won a gold medal at the 2015 World Championship, where he led all competitors with nine goals in 10 games.

The Seguins are a hockey family. Tyler's father, Paul, was a defenceman who captained his team at the University of Vermont. His mother and two younger sisters also play.

Tyler's minor hockey journey began in Whitby, Ontario, where he grew up, then shifted to the Toronto Nationals in Brampton. In 2008, he was selected ninth overall by the Plymouth Whalers in the OHL draft.

In his rookie season in 2008–09, Seguin started out with just one goal in his first 17 games before finding his form at the major junior level. He finished the year ranked second in Whalers scoring with 21 goals and 67 points and tied for the team's playoff scoring lead with 16 points in 11 games. The Whalers were eliminated by the eventual OHL and Memorial Cup champion Windsor Spitfires.

That second-round playoff series marked the first chapter in the competition that became known as "Taylor vs. Tyler." Spitfires winger Taylor Hall became Seguin's main rival for the first-overall spot in the 2010 NHL draft.

Determined to improve on his rookie season, Seguin dedicated himself to training and came back stronger in his draft year. He led the Spitfires and tied with Hall for the OHL scoring title with 106 points, but outscoring Hall in the goal column, 48–40. Both players were named to the OHL's first all-star team and Seguin also received the Red Tilson Trophy as the league's most outstanding player.

For the second straight year, the Whalers and Spitfires met in the second round of the OHL playoffs, and for the second straight year, Windsor prevailed — winning the OHL championship and a second-straight Memorial Cup. Seguin contributed five goals and 10 points in nine playoff games.

Midway through the 2009–10 season, NHL's Central Scouting ranked Hall first and Seguin second. When the final draft rankings were released in April, the players had switched positions — Seguin was now number one. He went on to impress league brass with his chiseled physique at May's draft combine in Toronto.

On draft day, Hall went first to the Edmonton Oilers and Seguin was chosen second by the Boston Bruins. The Bruins famously used a pick that they'd acquired as part of a trade that sent Phil Kessel to the Toronto Maple Leafs in September 2009.

Seguin made the jump to the NHL straight from junior, tallying 11 goals and 22 points in his rookie year on a deep Bruins team that finished first in the old Northeast Division with 103 points. His first NHL goal came in his second game, a 5–2 win over the Phoenix Coyotes.

In the playoffs, the inexperienced Seguin watched the first two rounds from the press box, but he saw game action in the Eastern Conference finals after an injury to teammate Patrice Bergeron.

Seguin scored a goal in his first career playoff game, a 5–2 loss to the Tampa Bay Lightning, then followed up with two goals and two assists in the Bruins' 6–5 win over the Lightning in Game 2. He was the first teenager to record four points in a playoff game since Trevor Linden did it with the Vancouver Canucks in 1989, and he was named the game's first star for his heroics.

The Bruins went on to beat the Lightning in seven games, then beat the Vancouver Canucks to capture the Stanley Cup. Altogether, Seguin recorded three goals and seven points in 13 playoff games.

In 2011–12, Seguin, playing right wing, became a regular in the lineup, a "top six" offensive threat who saw plenty of ice time on the power play. His sophomore season proved to be a breakout campaign: he finished the year as Boston's leader in goals (29), points (67), and game-winning goals (seven). Seguin also worked on the defensive side of his game, ultimately finishing with a plus-34 rating, which put him second in the NHL in plus-minus behind teammate Bergeron.

Despite a 102-point year and another first-place finish in the Northeast Division, the defending champion Bruins were eliminated by the Washington Capitals in the first round of the 2012 playoffs.

During the 2012–13 lockout, Seguin suited up for EHC Biel of the Swiss National League along with another NHL superstar, Patrick Kane. Though he played just 29 games with Biel, Seguin topped the team's year-end stats with 25 goals.

In December 2012, Seguin joined Canada's Spengler Cup team. He won more gold in his first international competition since the 2009 Ivan Hlinka Memorial Cup, where he had led his championship team in scoring as a 17-year-old.

When NHL play resumed in January 2013, Seguin put together another strong season, finishing second in team scoring with 16 goals in 48 games and tied for second with a plus-23 rating.

In the playoffs, Seguin recorded one goal and eight points in 22 games as the Bruins returned to the Stanley Cup finals before falling to the Chicago Blackhawks.

Shortly after the playoffs concluded, Seguin was hosting a Fourth of July party in Cape Cod when he got word that he was the centrepiece of a seven-player trade between the Bruins and the Dallas Stars. Seguin, Rich Peverley, and Ryan Button were shipped to the Stars for Loui Eriksson, Reilly Smith, Matt Fraser, and Joe Morrow.

Seguin had completed three successful seasons in Boston, but it was widely reported that the team's management was concerned with his exuberant off-ice lifestyle. After he got over the shock of the trade, it didn't take long for Seguin to adjust to his new surroundings in Dallas.

Seguin was moved back to centre and developed instant chemistry with new Stars captain Jamie Benn. Seguin recorded career bests in goals (37) and points (84) to finish fourth in NHL scoring in 2013–14. He followed up with another 37 goals in 2014–15 and finished seventh in league scoring, while his linemate Benn captured the Art Ross Trophy as the NHL's leading scorer with 87 points.

After the Stars failed to qualify for the 2015 playoffs, Seguin once again signed on with Team Canada, this time for the World Championship in Prague, Czech Republic. He scored a tournament-leading nine goals as Canada went unbeaten on its way to a gold medal.

In 2015–16, Seguin scored 33 goals and 73 points to finish 14th in league scoring, but he missed the last 10 games of the season with an Achilles tendon injury. With 109 points, the Stars finished the regular season in first place in the Western Conference, but a still-injured Seguin was able to play only one post-season game. The Stars fell to the St. Louis Blues in the second round.

Seguin joined Team Canada at the World Cup of Hockey in September 2016, but he suffered a heel injury in the first exhibition game, which kept him out of the lineup for the duration of the tournament.

Ready to start the season with Dallas in October, he played all 82 games. His 26 goals and 72 points ranked him 15th in the NHL, but he was nagged by the lingering effects of the Achilles injury. He also underwent surgery to repair a torn labrum in his right shoulder at the end of the season.

Like so many top teen prospects from the U.S. in the 21st century, Kevin Shattenkirk made his first move to the pros by joining USA Hockey's National Team Development Program. The 16-year-old signed on in 2005 and spent two years in Ann Arbor, Michigan, developing his young mind and body.

He helped the U.S. win a silver medal at the 2007 U18 World Championship in Tampere, Finland. Soon after, he was drafted 14th overall by Colorado at the 2007 NHL Entry Draft.

After graduating from the NTDP, he joined the Boston University Terriers in Hockey East, playing for three seasons and developing further. The defenceman's sophomore season was important. He played at the World Juniors midway through the year, and at the end of the season led the Terriers to an NCAA championship, assisting on Colby Cohen's overtime winner to defeat Miami University, 4–3, in the decisive game.

At the end of his third year, he and the Avs believed it was time to turn pro, so Shattenkirk signed a contract and said goodbye to BU in favour of a clear path to the NHL. He joined Colorado's AHL affiliate in Lake Erie, and after starting the 2010–11 season with the Monsters, he was called to the Avs. He never looked back.

## KEVIN SHATTENKIRK

B. NEW ROCHELLE, NEW YORK,
JANUARY 29, 1989
6'0" 209 LBS.
DEFENCE/SHOOTS RIGHT
DRAFTED 14TH OVERALL
BY COLORADO IN 2007
NHL DEBUT NOVEMBER 4, 2010
@SHATTDEUCES

Shattenkirk played 46 games with Colorado that year, but in a surprising move he found himself part of a large trade with St. Louis in February 2011. He, Chris Stewart, and a draft choice were traded for Erik Johnson, Jay McClement, and a draft. The Blues ended up missing the playoffs, but Shattenkirk joined the U.S. team for the World Championship in Slovakia.

He played more than six years with the Blues, becoming a dependable anchor on the blue line and averaging some 22 minutes a game. He played for his country again at the 2014 Olympics — an honour to be selected but a disappointing fourth-place result. His career highlight was surely in the spring of 2016 when the Blues made a terrific run to the conference finals, only to lose to San Jose in six games.

In summer 2013, he had signed a four-year, $17-million contract with St. Louis. But, as the 2016–17 season unfolded, it became clear to the Blues that he might be lost to free agency once it expired. The Blues had little choice but to trade him, to Washington, with Pheonix Copley for Zach Sanford, Brad Malone, and two draft choices.

Although Shattenkirk was going to a team that ended up first overall in the league, the Caps made an early playoff exit after losing to eventual champions Pittsburgh in seven games in the second round.

Nonetheless, Shattenkirk is a stud on the blue line and is the kind of defenceman every Cup-winning team needs.

When you think of Maurice Richard or Phil Esposito or Mike Bossy, you don't think, "Great passer, great vision, great speed." You think of one dimension only: Goal scorer. Wicked shot. Deadly around the net.

After a decade in the league, Steven Stamkos can be added to this list of names for the same reason. Only injury has prevented him from becoming arguably the greatest scorer of the 21st century so far. Even slowed by lost time, he has put the puck in the net with incredible consistency and skill.

Stamkos scored exactly 100 goals in 124 games with Sarnia in the OHL from 2006 to 2008, after which he was drafted first overall by Tampa Bay. From there, he made the NHL at age 18 and never looked back. The only trouble was that his coach with the Lightning, Barry Melrose, refused to support him. Stamkos got little ice time, scored less, and looked lost during the early part of his rookie season.

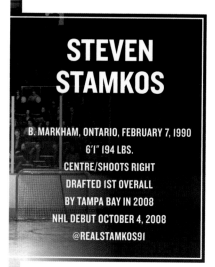

# STEVEN STAMKOS

B. MARKHAM, ONTARIO, FEBRUARY 7, 1990
6'1" 194 LBS.
CENTRE/SHOOTS RIGHT
DRAFTED 1ST OVERALL
BY TAMPA BAY IN 2008
NHL DEBUT OCTOBER 4, 2008
@REALSTAMKOS91

Not surprisingly, after Melrose was fired, Stamkos thrived. He finished his first year with 23 goals and, a year later, reached 53 to win his first Rocket Richard Trophy and establish himself as the league's newest scoring sensation. He followed with seasons of 45 and then 60 goals, winning his second Richard Trophy in 2011–12.

In 2012–13, he was slowed ever so slightly by the lockout, and he suffered a major injury early in the 2013–14 season when he crashed into the net and broke his leg. It was a double whammy. He was lost to the team for several months and, having been named to Canada's 2014 Olympic team, he missed the Sochi Games as well.

Stamkos had seasons of 43 and 36 goals in the two years leading up to his free agency. These lower numbers were not indicators of a declining player but a league in which scoring was nearing the impossible. Still, as July 1, 2016, approached, Toronto media went haywire in fanning the gossip flames suggesting he wanted to sign with his hometown team, the Leafs.

The noise drowned out reality, so when Stamkos signed an eight-year, $68-million contract with Tampa Bay two days before July 1, Toronto fans were stunned and incensed. However, on November 15, 2016, just a few weeks into his new contract, Stamkos fell awkwardly during a game and suffered a knee injury that kept him off the ice for the rest of the season.

Stamkos did finally play for Canada, at the 2016 World Cup before the 2016–17 season, winning the championship. Although he is only 27, he is in his 10th NHL season. He has 321 goals in just 586 regular-season games, putting him among the top scorers in the game. If he stays healthy, 500 is an easy target, and 600 or more is well within the realm of possibility. As goal scorers go, they don't get much better than "Stammer."

Late draft picks have been an occasional windfall in Canada's capital. Sixteen years after the Ottawa Senators selected Daniel Alfredsson in the sixth round of the NHL Entry Draft, the team used its 178th-overall pick in the same round to take Mark Stone, in 2010.

While no one expects Stone to fill the footsteps of Alfredsson — the former captain and long-time cornerstone of the franchise — the 6'3" right-winger has evolved from his humble beginnings in Winnipeg, Manitoba, to become one of the most important sparkplugs of the Senators offence.

After starring as a AAA midget with his hometown Thrashers, Stone had the good fortune of playing junior hockey in his native province with the Brandon Wheat Kings.

In his second WHL season, 2009–10, Stone netted 28 points in 39 regular-season games — and four points in 15 playoff games — en route to his team's appearance in the Memorial Cup. Brandon earned an automatic berth as the tournament hosts. Although the Wheat Kings defeated the WHL champion Calgary Hitmen in the semi-finals, they were no match for the powerhouse Windsor Spitfires in the championship game.

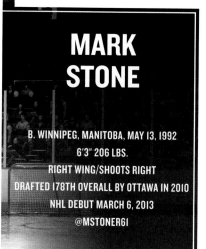

## MARK STONE

B. WINNIPEG, MANITOBA, MAY 13, 1992
6'3" 206 LBS.
RIGHT WING/SHOOTS RIGHT
DRAFTED 178TH OVERALL BY OTTAWA IN 2010
NHL DEBUT MARCH 6, 2013
@MSTONER61

The next year, Stone — now a newly drafted Senators prospect — cracked the 100-point barrier and earned a spot on the WHL Eastern Conference all-star team for his efforts. However, it was during Stone's final season of junior eligibility, 2011–12, that the player truly foreshadowed his greatness.

During the campaign, Stone averaged nearly two points a game, finishing with an astounding 41 goals and 82 assists in just 66 outings. He earned an invitation to play for Team Canada's entry at the World Junior Championship, hosted on home ice in Alberta. Stone led all Canadian players with 10 points in six games and was named one of the top three players on his team (along with Brandon Gormley and Brett Connolly). Canada settled for bronze at the tournament.

Stone capped off his illustrious junior career with a second consecutive all-star nomination in 2011–12, and he also won the Brad Hornung Trophy as the league's most sportsmanlike player. With the Wheat Kings eliminated from the playoffs, the Senators called upon Stone to make his NHL debut in Game 5 of Ottawa's first-round playoff series versus the New York Rangers. Stone collected an assist, threading the needle on a pass to Jason Spezza for the eventual game-winning marker.

In 2012–13, Stone had a brief four-game stint with the parent club in March, but he spent most of the season in the American Hockey League, toiling for the Binghamton Senators. He also used the following year to develop in the minor leagues, collecting 41 points in 37 games for

"Bingo." Stone managed to work his way into Ottawa's lineup for 19 games, and on January 4, 2014, he got the better of Carey Price for his first NHL goal.

Finally, in 2014–15, Stone earned a full-time spot on the Ottawa roster. He burst onto the big-league scene with 26 goals and 64 points in 80 games, finishing as the co-leader in rookie scoring with Calgary's Johnny Gaudreau. In a tight ballot at season's end, Stone was outvoted 1,147–1,078 for the Calder Trophy and wound up second to Florida's Aaron Ekblad.

There was no sophomore jinx to Stone's progression. He finished with 61 points in 75 games in his second pro season and got the call once again to play for Team Canada, at the 2016 World Championship. With a star-studded lineup that included Connor McDavid, Taylor Hall, and Matt Duchene, Canada successfully defended its gold medal.

The 2016–17 campaign had its share of triumphs and setbacks for Stone. He suffered a concussion in training camp but went on to play the bulk of the season before being felled by a leg injury in March. Stone finished the regular season with 54 points in 71 games, the fourth-highest total on the Sens.

Ottawa made a surprise run to the Eastern Conference finals in the spring of 2017, and in the second-round series against the New York Rangers, Stone scored pivotal goals both in Games 5 and 6 to help his team advance. But, still hobbled with a wonky leg, he had just one goal and an assist in the club's devastating seven-game loss to the Pittsburgh Penguins for the right to play for the Stanley Cup.

An accurate sharpshooter with a nose for the net, Stone has proven to be a late-round gem that the Senators were fortunate to unearth. And his best days might still be in the future.

Only a very few families have been blessed with the good fortune of producing several children talented enough to play at hockey's highest level. Most famously, the Sutter clan of Viking, Alberta, produced six siblings who played in the NHL: Brian, Darryl, Brent, Duane, Ron, and Rich. Thunder Bay, Ontario, is home to the four Staal brothers: Eric, Marc, Jordan, and Jaret.

Then there are the Strome brothers from Mississauga. Ryan, the eldest, has been a mentor to brothers Dylan, a first-round pick of the Arizona Coyotes, and Matthew, who entered his NHL draft year in 2017.

As a AAA minor midget player, Ryan starred for the Toronto Marlboros of the GTHL, the team that won the OHL Cup in 2008–09. He was on the radar of the Barrie Colts and was summarily selected by the junior club in the first round of the OHL Priority Selection Draft.

His stay in Barrie was short-lived. After 34 games, Strome was traded to Niagara in a deal involving star defenceman and St. Louis Blues prospect Alex Pietrangelo. Suiting up for Team Ontario at the 2010 World Hockey Challenge, Strome collected three points in six tournament games en route to a silver medal.

## RYAN STROME

B. MISSISSAUGA, ONTARIO, JULY 11, 1993
6'1" 199 LBS.
RIGHT WING/SHOOTS RIGHT
DRAFTED 5TH OVERALL
BY NY ISLANDERS IN 2011
NHL DEBUT DECEMBER 14, 2013
@STROME18

Strome's speed and keen hockey sense were assets in the player's meteoric rise in production in 2010–11. In a breakout season, Strome collected an amazing 33 goals and 106 points in only 65 regular-season games. He earned an invitation to play for Don Cherry's squad in the CHL Top Prospects Game, and at season's end, Strome was named as a Second Team OHL all-star.

The New York Islanders made Strome their first-round, fifth-overall selection at the NHL Entry Draft in June. After signing an entry-level contract at the beginning of the 2011–12 season, the highly touted prospect was returned to Niagara. In December, Strome took time away from his team to represent Canada at the 2012 World Junior Championship.

Playing in front of raucous crowds cheering for a gold medal on home ice in Calgary and Edmonton, the Canadians had a perfect preliminary round but lost to Russia in the semi-finals and were eventually left holding bronze. Strome and Jonathan Huberdeau each collected an impressive nine points in six tournament games, one point behind Mark Stone for the team lead.

Injuries limited Strome to just 46 regular-season games that year, but he appeared in all 20 of Niagara's playoff outings and collected 23 points. The Ice Dogs made it to the OHL finals before bowing out to London.

Before the end of the 2012 calendar year, Strome got to wear the maple leaf two more times. In the summer, he scored the overtime winner to decide the four-game Canada-Russia Under-20

Challenge. Then at Christmas, Strome joined Team Canada for his second consecutive World Junior appearance, playing on a squad that had a disappointing fourth-place finish.

Strome began the 2013–14 campaign with the Islanders' AHL affiliate, the Bridgeport Sound Tigers. He was finally called up to make his NHL debut on December 14. Just over three weeks later, Strome beat Dallas goalie Kari Lehtonen on a power play to score his first NHL goal. At season's end, Strome's NHL totals were a modest seven goals and 18 points in 37 games. The player's AHL output of 49 points was the best on the Sound Tigers, even though he appeared in only half of Bridgeport's games.

The next season, Strome became a full-time player for the Islanders. Skating on a team that finished with the third-best offence in the NHL, Strome played in 81 games in 2014–15. Generating scoring opportunities with his uncanny vision and playmaking, Strome had 17 goals and 50 points and finished third behind John Tavares and Kyle Okposo in team scoring. In the playoffs, Strome collected four points as the Islanders fell to Washington in a hard-fought seven-game series.

Strome took a backwards step in his production the following year, finding the back of the net just eight times in 71 games. The 2016–17 campaign featured turmoil within the Islanders' organization: coach Jack Capuano was fired and replaced by Doug Weight. Strome had suited up in every one of New York's games, but on March 22, he collided with Brady Skjei of the Rangers and sustained a season-ending wrist injury. At season's end, he was traded to Edmonton straight up for Jordan Eberle, where he started the 2017–18 season.

Given that he has two younger brothers moving up the pro ranks, perhaps the sibling rivalry will provide the eldest Strome with further motivation to regain the form he displayed as a junior.

In this age of Twitter and Facebook and Instagram, there is perhaps no hockey player who is more of a self-promoter than P.K. Subban, but his skill on ice cannot be denied. First in Montreal and now in Nashville, he is a polarizing figure — you either love him . . . or you don't.

Subban grew up in Toronto but always loved *les Canadiens*. As a teen, he played junior hockey for Belleville for four years starting in 2005. A defenceman, Subban loved rushing the puck, but defensively he was a liability — his offensive forays often leading to turnovers and good scoring chances the other way.

As good fortune had it, the Habs drafted Subban 43rd overall in 2007 after his second season with the Bulls. He went back to junior for two more years to develop his game, and both years he played for Canada at the mid-season World Junior Championship, winning gold both times.

Subban spent most of 2009–10 with Montreal's AHL affiliate in Hamilton, but he did play his first two NHL games with the Habs during a brief call-up. At season's end, he was recalled again and played during the Habs' playoff run, which went two series. He made the team full-time at training camp in 2010 and has been in the NHL ever since.

## P.K. SUBBAN

B. TORONTO, ONTARIO, MAY 13, 1989
6'0" 210 LBS.
DEFENCE/SHOOTS RIGHT
DRAFTED 43RD OVERALL
BY MONTREAL IN 2007
NHL DEBUT FEBRUARY 12, 2010
@PKSUBBAN1

Although he developed quickly, the noise around him detracted from his focus on the game. Opinionated and a lover of the attention Montreal media happily gave him, he spoke loud and often, but on ice he was learning how to maintain an offensive presence while shoring up his play in his own end.

By 2012–13, he had a fine season and was named Norris Trophy winner. A year later, as a restricted free agent, he signed an eight-year, $72-million contract, making him the highest-paid defenceman in the league. There was a twist, though: the deal called for a no-trade clause to take effect on July 1, 2016.

The Canadiens were getting tired of Subban's need for attention, and two days before the no-trade clause kicked in, they traded him to Nashville for blueliner Shea Weber. Many believed the Habs made a sensational move, getting a power defenceman with the hardest shot in the game and getting rid of, essentially, an off-ice problem.

That might have been true, but Subban got the last laugh. While the Habs were eliminated in the first round of the 2017 playoffs, Subban's Predators advanced to the Stanley Cup finals, losing to Pittsburgh in six games.

Subban was his old self, though. As much as his sensational play helped the Preds get so far, he taunted Sidney Crosby towards the end of the series, which is widely regarded as the motivation Pittsburgh's 87 used to play at an unmatched level in the final games to lead the Penguins to victory.

Love him or hate him, Subban is a unique and not unwelcome addition to the NHL — he is seldom boring and has proven to be a winner at every level of play.

When a generational talent scores seemingly at will and becomes a human highlight reel, the superlatives to describe the player's jaw-dropping goals become almost cliché. Indeed, fans who flock to the Scottrade Center in St. Louis have the luxury of knowing that every night there may be an opportunity to witness a spectacular play made by the Blues' scoring sensation, Vladimir Tarasenko.

Blessed with superb stickhandling ability and laser-sharp shooting accuracy, Tarasenko was born with hockey in his blood. His father, Andrei, enjoyed a playing career in Russia that spanned two decades, highlighted by an appearance at the 1994 Winter Olympics in Lillehammer, Norway.

The younger Tarasenko made his first appearance on the international stage at the 2009 U18 World Championship, starring on a Russian team that finished with a silver medal. Tarasenko collected a remarkable eight goals and 15 points in a mere seven games and was named to the tournament all-star team.

In a deep 2010 NHL Entry Draft that was highlighted by top picks Taylor Hall and Tyler Seguin, the Blues found their own jewel with their first-round, 16th-overall pick in Tarasenko. The prospect went on to develop his game for the next three seasons under the guidance of his father, and coach, for the KHL team Sibir in Novosibirsk.

# VLADIMIR TARASENKO

B. YAROSLAVL, SOVIET UNION (RUSSIA),
DECEMBER 13, 1991
6'0" 219 LBS.
RIGHT WING/SHOOTS LEFT
DRAFTED 16TH OVERALL BY ST. LOUIS IN 2010
NHL DEBUT JANUARY 19, 2013
@TARA9191

Tarasenko also represented Russia at two World Junior Championships. In 2010, he played for a squad that finished a disappointing sixth. But in 2011, Tarasenko captained a team that staged the biggest comeback in the tournament's history: Russia snagged the gold medal from the grasp of Team Canada.

Trailing 3–0 in the third period of the championship game, Russia stormed back with three goals to even the score, Tarasenko firing the equalizer past the stunned goaltender, Mark Visentin. Canada — playing in front of a legion of fans who had made the cross-border trek to Buffalo, New York — never recovered, and Russia won 5–3. For the tournament, Tarasenko registered seven goals and four assists in seven games.

Four months later, Tarasenko, still just 19 years old, played for his country at the senior World Championship, barely missing the podium with a fourth-place finish.

The NHL finally got its first glimpse of Tarasenko during the lockout-shortened 2012–13 season. The Blues rookie made his debut on January 19 against Detroit and sent the fans home happy with a two-goal effort. His first NHL tally came just 6:36 into the game, versus Red Wings netminder Jimmy Howard.

Two nights later, in Nashville, Tarasenko had a goal and two assists. Five points in two games

was undoubtedly an auspicious beginning to his North American pro career. Tarasenko finished the campaign with 19 points in 38 games and received lukewarm consideration for the Calder Trophy, getting a mere 0.67 percent of the vote to finish 12th in the balloting.

Tarasenko avoided a sophomore jinx, however, netting 21 goals the following year. He was named to the Olympic roster where he had the opportunity to play in the Winter Games on home ice in Sochi. The Russians never found their collective legs and finished in fifth place.

It was during Tarasenko's third NHL season, 2014–15, that the player made the transition from budding prospect to superstar. During a visit to New York's Madison Square Garden on November 3, Tarasenko scored an unbelievable goal against the Rangers that, just as remarkably, has become a trademark of his career.

On a Blues power play, Tarasenko sped into the New York zone, accelerating past defender Mike Kostka and between winger Rick Nash and defenceman Dylan McIlrath. Tarasenko deftly circled around McIlrath and found himself one-on-one against goalie Cam Talbot. Moving from his forehand to his backhand, Tarasenko skillfully tucked the puck into the net with one hand on the stick. The mesmerized Rangers could only watch in awe.

Tarasenko finished with 37 goals and 73 points in his breakout year. He earned a silver medal with Russia at the 2015 World Championship and, at season's end, he was named to the first of two consecutive all-star teams at right wing.

Befuddling goalies and defenders with his explosive speed and tremendous skill, Tarasenko registered 74 and 75 points, respectively, in his next two seasons, representing Russia again at the 2016 World Cup of Hockey.

At any given moment, a Tarasenko goal could easily become an internet sensation.

Such was the promise of John Tavares that his family petitioned Hockey Canada to have him considered for exceptional player status so that he could play major junior hockey a year early. The request was granted, and so Tavares, at age 14, became the youngest player ever drafted into the OHL.

He joined the Oshawa Generals in the fall of 2005 (at age 15) and started a career that continues to be of the highest quality. In his first season, he scored 45 goals in 65 games and was named rookie of the year. The next year, he had a whopping 72 goals in 67 games and was named the CHL's most valuable player.

But because he was born on September 20, five days after the date set by the NHL for draft eligibility, Tavares wasn't selected until 2009. He played two more years of junior and, by the time he was done, he had scored 215 career goals in junior, the most ever.

Although he never won the Memorial Cup, he represented Canada several times in junior. His first event was the U18 World Championship in 2006, followed by consecutive World Junior tournaments in 2008 and 2009, both resulting in Canada winning gold.

## JOHN TAVARES

B. MISSISSAUGA, ONTARIO,
SEPTEMBER 20, 1990
6'1" 211 LBS.
CENTRE/SHOOTS LEFT
DRAFTED 1ST OVERALL
BY NY ISLANDERS IN 2009
NHL DEBUT OCTOBER 3, 2009
@91TAVARES

There was no question Tavares would go first overall in the draft; the only question was which team would earn the right. It turned out to be the New York Islanders, a once-proud team that had fallen on tough times. Tavares made the team at his first training camp in 2009 at age 19 and showed no signs of having difficulty coping with the highest level of play.

Not the smoothest skater, he had great knack around the goal and great vision with the puck. He was also the kind of player who lifted the play of those around him, so it was no surprise that he scored 24 goals and 54 points as a rookie or that the team became more competitive than it had been in some time.

Although the Isles missed the playoffs each of his first three seasons, he used the early finish to play for Canada at the World Championships. These experiences helped cement his place on Canada's Olympic team for Sochi in 2014, but Tavares suffered a knee injury and didn't play after the quarter-finals; the team went on to win a gold medal.

Back in the NHL, Tavares reached 38 goals and 86 points in 2014–15. He had been named captain in the summer of 2013, and he is clearly the face of a team that continues to struggle, now at its new arena in Brooklyn, and with its leaders who have yet to provide a supporting cast for "JT."

Quite simply one of the best players in the game, Tavares is set to become a free agent on July 1, 2018. The Isles may lock him up with a big contract if he is impressed by the team's direction, or he may head to more Cup-contending pastures where his skills might serve a greater purpose.

One of the players who ushered in hockey's new generation, Jonathan Toews boasts speed and skill but is best known for his leadership as part of a long list of winning teams.

Toews enjoyed great success early in his career. He was just 22 when he became the youngest member of the esteemed Triple Gold Club, with a Stanley Cup to go along with his gold medals from the Olympics and the World Championship.

Born in Winnipeg, Manitoba, and raised in a bilingual family, Toews spent two years playing midget prep at Shattuck-St. Mary's, a boarding school in Minnesota known as the "Hogwarts of Hockey." He posted 64 goals and 118 points in 2003–04 and added 110 points in his senior year as he helped his team win a national championship.

In January 2005, Toews got his first taste of international hockey gold as he captained Canada West to a win and was named MVP at the World U17 Hockey Challenge in Lethbridge, Alberta.

After graduating from high school, Toews signed on at the University of North Dakota, helping his team reach the Frozen Four in both of his seasons in Grand Forks. He was part of Canada's gold-medal winning team at the 2006 World Junior Championship as a 17-year-old, then returned as an alternate captain to claim a second gold medal in 2007.

When his high-school season was over, Toews signed on to join the Canadian men's World Championship team in Moscow, Russia. He posted seven points in nine games as Canada beat out Finland for the gold medal.

In June 2006, Toews was drafted third overall by the Chicago Blackhawks. One year later, he made the jump to the NHL, joining a team that had appeared in just one playoff series in the previous nine seasons.

## JONATHAN TOEWS

B. WINNIPEG, MANITOBA, APRIL 29, 1988
6'2" 201 LBS.
CENTRE/SHOOTS LEFT
DRAFTED 3RD OVERALL BY CHICAGO IN 2006
NHL DEBUT OCTOBER 10, 2007
@JONATHANTOEWS

Toews was one of two standout rookies to join the Blackhawks for the 2007–08 season, along with 2007 first-overall pick Patrick Kane. Toews scored 24 goals and added 30 assists in his first NHL campaign; the Blackhawks improved by 17 points in the Central Division standings but fell three points short of a post-season berth. Toews placed third in the voting for the Calder Trophy, which went to Kane.

At the end of the 2007–08 season, Toews once again joined Team Canada for the World Championship, adding a silver medal to his collection after the Canadians fell to Russia in overtime in the gold-medal game in Quebec City.

After wearing an "A" in his rookie season, Toews was named Blackhawks team captain at 20 years old on July 18, 2008 — the third-youngest captain in NHL history at that time, behind Sidney Crosby and Vincent Lecavalier.

Wearing the "C," he improved to 34 goals and 69 points in his sophomore campaign and started to gain notice for his strong two-way play. The Blackhawks improved by another 16 points in the standings in 2008–09 to qualify for the playoffs. They won their first playoff series since 1996 and reached the Western Conference finals. It was but a sign of things to come.

In the 2009–10 season, Toews's output held steady at 68 points, but the Blackhawks moved up another notch in the standings, finishing with 112 points. It was their first division title since 1993, when they were in the old Norris Division.

Toews also earned his first invitation to the Olympics in 2010, where he led Team Canada with eight points and scored the opening goal of Canada's gold-medal win over Team USA. Only 21 years old, Toews was voted to the tournament all-star team and received the Directorate Award for Best Forward.

After his success at the Olympics, Toews didn't ease up when he returned to his day job, leading the Blackhawks to their first Stanley Cup since 1961. Chicago's playoff route went through Nashville, Vancouver, and San Jose before the Blackhawks beat the Philadelphia Flyers in six games of the Cup finals.

Toews finished with a team-leading 29 points, including three game-winning goals, and he was awarded the Conn Smythe Trophy as the most valuable player in the post-season.

Toews, 22, and Kane, 21, had been in the NHL for just three seasons but had already established themselves among the best in the game. Though salary-cap issues meant that the Blackhawks lost key players from their Cup-winning roster, Toews and Kane combined with Marian Hossa, Duncan Keith, and Brent Seabrook to form a nucleus to lead the team to more success in the years that followed.

In 2010–11, Toews reached a new career high with 76 points and became a first-time finalist for the Frank Selke Trophy as the NHL's best defensive forward, but the Blackhawks were eliminated from the Stanley Cup playoffs in the first round, a seven-game overtime shocker at the hands of the Vancouver Canucks.

During the 2011–12 season, Toews continued to produce at nearly a point-a-game pace, but he missed the last 22 games of the regular season due to post-concussion symptoms. He returned for the playoffs, but once again the Blackhawks were eliminated in the first round, this time by the Phoenix Coyotes.

The lockout-shortened 2012–13 season marked the pinnacle of the Blackhawks' success. The team went through the first half of the 48-game schedule before recording a regulation loss, posting a 21-0-3 record, and the Blackhawks finished atop the league standings for the first time since 1990–91, with 77 points.

That set the stage for playoff wins over the Minnesota Wild, Detroit Red Wings, and the defending champion Los Angeles Kings. In the Stanley Cup finals, the Blackhawks beat the Boston Bruins, 4–2, to capture another title.

Toews tied for the Chicago team lead with 23 goals in the regular season and finished fourth in Hart Trophy voting for the NHL's most valuable player. He was awarded the Selke Trophy.

The Blackhawks' hopes of repeating as Stanley Cup champions were dashed at the end of the 2013–14 season, thanks to a Game 7 overtime loss to the eventual champion Los Angeles Kings in the second round. Toews did add a second Olympic gold medal to his collection in Sochi in February 2014, once again scoring the opening goal for Canada in the championship game.

In the 2014–15 season, his seventh as Chicago's captain, Toews was named the winner of the Mark Messier Leadership Award and the Blackhawks captured their third Stanley Cup in six seasons, beating out the Nashville Predators, Minnesota Wild, Anaheim Ducks, and Tampa Bay Lightning.

By the time he was handed the Stanley Cup for the third time by NHL Commissioner Gary Bettman on June 15, 2015, the player known throughout his career as "Captain Serious" had matured from a young superstar into a seasoned veteran, with more on his mind that just the game of hockey. Away from the rink, he is often to be found with a self-improvement book in hand, and he has become a vocal supporter of the fight against climate change.

Before the beginning of the 2016–17 season, Toews participated in another championship with Team Canada, at the World Cup of Hockey in Toronto. Toews recorded five points in six tournament games, scoring the game-winning goal against Team Europe in the round-robin portion of the tournament, then setting up Brad Marchand's short-handed tournament winner in the final series.

Now a mature 29, Captain Serious is in the tough position of having done everything one might want to accomplish in a career and having to find the internal drive to continue to accomplish more. If anyone can, though, it's Toews.

Growing up in two gritty industrial towns in the U.S., Vincent Trocheck pursued a career in the game, though a chance at playing in the NHL was never a sure thing. Born in Pittsburgh, he moved to Detroit at age 13 and then played in nearby Saginaw with the OHL's Spirit at age 16.

By no means the biggest player, Trocheck fought for every puck and worked his butt off to create every scoring opportunity. He wasn't a star on day one, but after four full years in the OHL, he was certainly a bona fide NHL prospect.

Trocheck was drafted 64th overall by Florida in 2011 at the end of his second year of junior. Some third-round choices make the grade but many don't, which is why Trocheck continued to give it his all in junior. It wasn't until his final year that he was selected by USA Hockey to play at the World Junior Championship, and he made the most of his chance in 2013 in Ufa, Russia.

He assisted on the tying goal and scored into the empty net to seal a 3–1 win over Sweden for gold, an unexpected title for the young team and new coach (Buffalo Sabres bench boss Phil Housley).

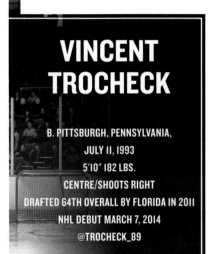

# VINCENT TROCHECK

B. PITTSBURGH, PENNSYLVANIA,
JULY 11, 1993
5'10" 182 LBS.
CENTRE/SHOOTS RIGHT
DRAFTED 64TH OVERALL BY FLORIDA IN 2011
NHL DEBUT MARCH 7, 2014
@TROCHECK_89

Playing much of 2013–14 with San Antonio, Florida's AHL affiliate, Trocheck had 42 points in 55 games before earning a call-up to the Panthers. In 20 games down the stretch, he had five goals, and by the next year he was ready for The Show on a nightly basis.

Despite a middling rookie season in which he managed only seven goals in 50 games, Trocheck was clearly a prospect with enough upside to be given a lengthy shot at making it. He rewarded the Panthers' patience by scoring 25 goals and 53 points in 2015–16, and a year later he had 23 goals and 54 points.

The management group that put together Team North America for the 2016 World Cup had no problem adding Trocheck to the lineup. Although he managed only one goal in three games, he was a solid contributor whose speed made him as much a part of the team as any other player on the super-fast Under-24 roster.

As with many small players who make it to the NHL, Trocheck can pinpoint his success to many attributes which are, in fact, the result of being small. He works tirelessly on his shot and has speed to burn. He is tenacious and opportunistic and has great hockey sense. He can play at both ends of the ice, with or without the puck, and is not prone to selfish play or lazy mistakes. You'll never mistake him for McDavid or Matthews, but he is a star in a fast league who has plenty of life left in his game yet.

Jacob Trouba has developed into one of the game's most effective shutdown defencemen. Patrolling the blue line of the Winnipeg Jets, Trouba exhibits a style characterized by aggression, grit, and toughness.

Trouba was recruited into USA Hockey's National Team Development Program as a 16-year-old and earned immediate success representing his country. The Rochester, Michigan, native won back-to-back gold medals with the United States at the U18 World Championship in 2011 and 2012. In the latter year, he also made an appearance at the World Junior Championship. The Americans could do no better than seventh, but Trouba's stock was rising.

The player cracked the top 10 among North American skaters in the rankings issued by the Central Scouting Bureau. Sure enough, at the 2012 NHL Entry Draft, the Winnipeg Jets selected Trouba ninth overall. That fall, Trouba suited up as a freshman for the University of Michigan, playing under legendary coach Red Berenson. He went on to register 12 goals and 29 points in 37 games with the Wolverines; however, his greatest accomplishment that season came overseas.

## JACOB TROUBA

B. ROCHESTER, MICHIGAN,
FEBRUARY 26, 1994
6'3" 202 LBS.
DEFENCE/SHOOTS RIGHT
DRAFTED 9TH OVERALL BY WINNIPEG IN 2012
NHL DEBUT OCTOBER 1, 2013
@JACOBTROUBA

Ufa, Russia, played host to the 2013 U20 tournament, and Trouba laced up the skates for the red, white, and blue at the event for the second year in a row. Coached by Sabres bench boss Phil Housley and stocked with blue-chip prospects such as Trouba, Alex Galchenyuk, and Shayne Gostisbehere, the Americans rebounded from a mediocre preliminary round to win three straight playoff games en route to the gold medal.

Trouba was outstanding, collecting four goals and nine points in seven games. He was recognized with the Directorate Award for the tournament's best defenceman.

Just four months later, there was more hardware to be earned. In May, Trouba was off to Scandinavia for the senior World Championship, co-hosted by Sweden and Finland. Thanks to a shootout-winning goal by international junior teammate Galchenyuk, the United States edged the Finns in a shootout to claim a rare bronze medal in the tournament.

In the fall of 2013, Trouba earned a spot on the Jets roster out of training camp. He made the most of his NHL debut in an October 1 road game in Edmonton, collecting a goal and an assist versus goaltender Devan Dubnyk. The Jets outlasted the Oilers, 5–4.

Impressively, Trouba amassed 10 goals and 29 points in 65 games during his rookie season. Nathan MacKinnon of the Colorado Avalanche was the runaway Calder Trophy winner, but Trouba was among a group of young defenders — including Boston's Torey Krug and Pittsburgh's Olli Maatta — who received a fair share of third- and fourth-place votes.

Over the next two seasons, Trouba's production remained consistent, albeit lower than expected, finishing at 22 and 21 points, respectively. In the summer of 2016, he joined a star-studded group of young players on Team North America at the World Cup of Hockey.

Despite the honour of being named to the team, there was the matter of Trouba's contract which was still up in the air. The player's three-year, entry-level deal had expired. Complicating the situation, Trouba had found difficulty under Winnipeg coach Paul Maurice in getting enough ice time warranted by a top-four defenceman who shoots right. Jets blueliners Dustin Byfuglien and Tyler Myers were ahead of Trouba on the depth chart. As a result, Trouba requested a trade while sitting out the first six weeks of the season.

The stalemate came to an end in the first week of November. Trouba signed a two-year, $6-million contract with Winnipeg and finally returned to the lineup on November 11.

Controversy ensued during a Jets eastern road trip in February. In Pittsburgh, Winnipeg's Blake Wheeler was on the receiving end of a hit to the head from Penguins sniper Evgeni Malkin. Three nights later, when the Jets paid a visit to Ottawa, Trouba delivered a shoulder-to-head hit on Senators forward Mark Stone and received a two-game suspension by the NHL. The ruling drew the ire of Maurice and the Jets, who couldn't help but wonder whether the similar incident with Malkin was allowed to escape supplemental discipline because of the Pittsburgh forward's superstar status.

Despite playing in only 60 games as a result of his contract dispute, Trouba posted career highs in assists (25), points (33), and average time on ice (24:58) during the 2016–17 season.

A physical rearguard whose game continues to develop, Trouba has ample opportunity to establish himself as an elite defender in the league.

A veteran leader and owner of the NHL's hardest shot, Shea Weber is best described as an old-school defenceman.

Weber is a man of strong character but few words, who prefers to let his play do the talking. On the ice, he's a three-time Norris Trophy finalist and a two-time Olympic gold medallist.

The Nashville Predators got a diamond in the rough when they selected Weber 49th overall in the second round of the 2003 draft. He's a native of Sicamous, British Columbia — a tiny community with a population of 1,786, which has produced an impressive list of NHL players, including Kris Beech (drafted 1999), Colin Fraser (drafted 2003), and Cody Franson (drafted 2005).

Playing in a small town, Weber flew under the radar during his minor hockey years. He wasn't selected in the WHL's bantam draft but was added to the Kelowna Rockets' protected list after Kelowna's assistant general manager Lorne Frey noticed him while scouting two of his teammates in a bantam game during the 2000–01 season — Weber's first year as a full-time defenceman.

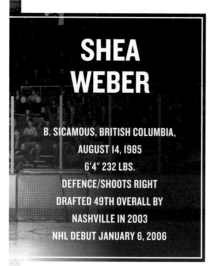

**SHEA WEBER**

B. SICAMOUS, BRITISH COLUMBIA,
AUGUST 14, 1985
6'4" 232 LBS.
DEFENCE/SHOOTS RIGHT
DRAFTED 49TH OVERALL BY
NASHVILLE IN 2003
NHL DEBUT JANUARY 6, 2006

Frey was impressed with Weber's skating and his grit; at that point, he already had good size. By the time Weber was 15, he had shot up to 6'2" and still had more growing to do.

At 16, Weber attended the Rockets training camp in the fall of 2001. He played five WHL games before being returned to his hometown Junior B Sicamous Eagles of the Kootenay International Junior Hockey League. Weber recorded 42 points in 47 games as the Eagles built a record of 43-5-1-1 before winning the KIJHL's league championship and the Western Canadian Junior B championship, the Keystone Cup.

In the 2002–03 season, Weber made the full-time jump to the Rockets and once again was part of a championship team as Kelowna captured its first WHL title in franchise history. In his first major junior season, Weber's calling card was his toughness: he led his team with 167 penalty minutes, the highest total of his career.

Draft eligible just weeks after appearing in the Memorial Cup, Weber had yet to develop the potent slap shot that would become his trademark in the NHL. He had scored just two goals and added 18 assists during the regular season, then added one goal and four assists in 19 playoff games.

The Predators took their time in bringing Weber along to the NHL level. After being drafted, he started to develop when he was returned to Kelowna for two additional seasons. Weber scored 12 goals both years, top among Rockets defencemen, while Kelowna continued to dominate the WHL.

In 2003–04, the Rockets finished first in the league's regular-season standings and set a WHL record for defence that still stands, allowing just 125 goals in 72 games. Kelowna failed to repeat

as playoff champions after being eliminated by the Everett Silvertips in the Western Conference finals, but the team still qualified for the Memorial Cup tournament as the host.

The Rockets won the Memorial Cup on home ice with a 2–1 win over the Gatineau Olympiques. Weber finished the playoffs with three goals and 17 points in 17 games and was named to the WHL's second all-star team.

As a 19-year-old, Weber had his best offensive season in the WHL; in 2004–05, he finished the year with 12 goals and 41 points in 60 games. His offensive flair started to take centre stage in the playoffs, where he contributed nine goals and 17 points in 18 games. He was named playoff MVP as he won his second WHL championship, but the Rockets fell short in their quest to repeat as Memorial Cup champions.

Weber also participated in his first international tournament during the 2004–05 season, winning gold with Team Canada at the 2005 World Junior Championship in Grand Forks, North Dakota.

His junior career complete, Weber started his first pro season with the AHL's Milwaukee Admirals but was soon called up by the Predators. He played his first NHL game on January 6, 2006. Weber finished his rookie year with 12 goals and 27 points in 46 games in Milwaukee and 10 points in 28 regular-season games in Nashville. He then appeared in four playoff games with the Predators before rejoining the Admirals for their run to the Calder Cup finals.

After that, Weber never played another game in the AHL. He became a full-time Nashville Predators blueliner in 2006–07 and quickly established himself as an offensive threat, scoring 17 goals to finish tied for fifth in the NHL in scoring by defencemen. Weber capped off his season with a trip to Moscow, where he earned another gold medal as part of Team Canada at the 2007 World Championship.

Two years later, Weber scored 23 goals for the first time to join the conversation as one of the league's top blueliners. He finished fourth in Norris Trophy voting in the 2008–09 season and subsequently was named runner-up for the Norris in 2010–11 and 2011–12. He finished third in voting in 2013–14.

Once again, Weber signed on with Team Canada at the World Championship in May 2009 after the Predators were eliminated in the Stanley Cup playoffs. He brought home a silver medal from Berne, Switzerland, and was named the tournament's best defenceman, leading all blueliners with four goals and 12 points in nine games.

In 2010, the international platform was once again the highlight of Weber's season. In his home province of British Columbia, he skated to gold with Team Canada at the Olympic Winter Games in Vancouver. Finishing second among all defencemen with six points in seven games, he was also named to the tournament all-star team.

Weber went on to win more gold with Canada at the 2014 Olympics in Sochi, Russia, and played on Canada's winning team at the 2016 World Cup of Hockey, but the Stanley Cup has continued to elude him. In 12 NHL seasons, he has yet to play past the second round. Weber's best playoffs to date were with the Predators in 2015–16, when he recorded three goals and seven points in 14 games before Nashville fell to the San Jose Sharks in Game 7 of the conference semi-finals.

On July 19, 2012, Weber signed an offer sheet with the Philadelphia Flyers that would have earned him a contract worth $110 million over 14 years, including an up-front signing bonus of $68 million. The Predators matched the offer five days later, keeping him in Nashville.

Weber was awarded the captaincy in Nashville at the beginning of the 2010–11 season. He kept the "C" for six years before being dealt to the Montreal Canadiens for fellow defenceman P.K. Subban, on June 29, 2016. In his first season in Montreal, Weber's 17 goals and 42 points led all Canadiens blueliners and ranked him fifth overall in team scoring.

In recent years, Weber has also taken over top spot among the NHL's hardest shooters. He fell just short of Zdeno Chara's record of 108.8 miles per hour when he won the hardest shot competition at the All-Star Game in 2015 with a blast of 108.5 miles per hour. In 2016, he defended his title with a shot of 108.1 miles per hour, and in 2017, he won a third straight title at a comparatively modest 102.8 miles per hour.

A crafty playmaker with excellent hockey sense, Alexander Wennberg rose to the top of the depth chart at centre for the Columbus Blue Jackets by his third North American pro season. Impressively, he has managed to have a relatively penalty-free career, compiling a scant 45 PIMs in his first 217 NHL games.

The Stockholm native starred as a junior with the Djurgarden U18 team. He first donned the blue-and-gold colours of Sweden at the 2012 U18 World Championship, playing on a team that won the silver medal. Wennberg had a phenomenal tournament: he posted three goals and six assists in six games.

The 2012–13 season marked Wennberg's first year of Swedish professional hockey. Only 18 years old, he suited up for the senior Djurgarden club, a roster that employed several young players as a result of the NHL lockout. Wennberg registered 32 points in 46 games while taking time off in late December to represent Sweden at the World Junior Championship.

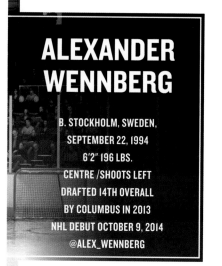

## ALEXANDER WENNBERG

B. STOCKHOLM, SWEDEN,
SEPTEMBER 22, 1994
6'2" 196 LBS.
CENTRE / SHOOTS LEFT
DRAFTED 14TH OVERALL
BY COLUMBUS IN 2013
NHL DEBUT OCTOBER 9, 2014
@ALEX_WENNBERG

The Swedes had a formidable squad that also included future NHLers Filip Forsberg, Viktor Arvidsson, and Rickard Rakell, but the United States was the better team in the final game, posting a 3–1 victory to win the gold medal.

The 2013 NHL Entry Draft featured a Scandinavian storyline. Four months earlier, the Columbus Blue Jackets had fired general manager Scott Howson and named Jarmo Kekalainen as his replacement. Kekalainen, a native of Tampere, Finland, thus became the first European GM in league history. With his first-ever selection in his role, Kekalainen picked Wennberg for the Jackets, 14th overall.

Wennberg returned to Sweden in the fall for one final junior season, playing 50 games for Frolunda during which he notched 16 goals and 21 points. He made a return to the World Junior tournament and experienced the once-in-a-lifetime opportunity to play for a gold medal on home ice in Malmo, Sweden.

But the host country had its hopes shattered by neighbouring rival Finland and was forced to settle for silver after a 3–2 overtime loss in the final game. Wennberg registered seven points in as many outings over the two weeks.

In May 2014, Wennberg signed an entry-level contract with the Blue Jackets. He cracked the lineup coming out of the fall training camp and collected an assist in his NHL debut on October 9 against Buffalo. Altogether, Wennberg played 68 games in his rookie year and produced a respectable four goals, 16 assists, and 20 points.

In a quirky numerical twist, Wennberg's sophomore season of 2015–16 saw an exact two-fold increase in each of the three offensive categories: an output of eight goals, 32 assists, and

40 points. The player's gentlemanly style of play was exemplified by his tiny total of just two penalty minutes in 69 games — a single minor infraction for holding in the team's 78th game of the season.

At the 2016 World Championship, Wennberg joined a Tre Kronor squad that included countryman Gustav Nyquist of the Detroit Red Wings. They both compiled eight points in as many games to lead their team in scoring.

A turning point in Wennberg's development occurred when Columbus pulled the trigger on a major mid-season trade, sending centre Ryan Johansen to Nashville for defenceman Seth Jones. The transaction afforded the opportunity for Wennberg to establish himself as the team's top pivot, and he took full advantage.

In 2016–17, Wennberg centred a line with Brandon Saad and Nick Foligno that became Columbus's most productive forward unit. He roared out of the gate with 19 points in his first 20 games of the year, a stretch of play that was highlighted by a career-best four-point effort on November 4. On that day, Wennberg recorded four assists as Columbus routed goalie Al Montoya and the Montreal Canadiens, 10–0.

Wennberg went on to lead the Blue Jackets with 46 assists that season and finished with 59 points, second-best on the team only to Cam Atkinson. Wennberg had a rare break in his pacifist nature on December 16 when — in defence of teammate Saad — he dropped the gloves against Calgary's Matthew Tkachuk for his first NHL fight.

The Blue Jackets had a surprise 50-win campaign, highlighted by a 16-game winning streak, and Wennberg was an integral part of Columbus's success. Indeed, he will be called upon to continue to spark the club's offence for the foreseeable future.

Columbus Blue Jackets fans might not be thrilled to know that their young power-play quarterback grew up as a fan of the rival Detroit Red Wings. But Zach Werenski could hardly have picked a better role model than seven-time Norris Trophy–winning defenceman Nicklas Lidstrom.

Like the legendary Swede, Werenski has a steady work ethic that's paid off with the machine-like efficiency of his game. Growing up near Detroit as the son of a policeman, he played minor hockey in the Little Caesars and Belle Tire programs. The smooth-skating blueliner's talent was apparent early on, and he headed to nearby Ann Arbor to spend a year with USA Hockey's National Team Development Program (NTDP). Werenski established himself as a force with the U17 team but also played four games with the U18 team at age 16.

However, instead of returning to the NTDP the following season, he decided to enroll at the University of Michigan. That challenged him academically as well as hockey-wise. Werenski split his summer between studying physics and English and training for the upcoming season.

## ZACH WERENSKI

B. GROSSE POINTE, MICHIGAN, JULY 19, 1997
6'2" 218 LBS.
DEFENCE/SHOOTS LEFT
DRAFTED 8TH OVERALL
BY COLUMBUS IN 2015
NHL DEBUT OCTOBER 13, 2016
@ZACHWERENSKI

The plan worked out well for the freshman as he led the Wolverines defencemen in scoring with 25 points in 35 games. Additionally, he suited up for the fifth-place U.S. World Junior team in Montreal. He was one of just three 1997-born players, along with Noah Hanifin and Auston Matthews, to make the team.

Werenski's rapid progress attracted Columbus GM Jarmo Kekalainen and his staff. Could he turn out to be the next Lidstrom? Getting picked eighth overall made him the third defenceman taken in 2015 after Hanifin (fifth, Carolina) and Ivan Provorov (seventh, Philadelphia). And Werenski continued to blossom in his sophomore year at Michigan, scoring 36 points in 36 games. He also stepped up at the 2016 World Juniors in Finland, leading all blueliners with nine points as the Americans took bronze. He was named Best Defenceman by the IIHF Directorate and made the tournament all-star team.

It would have been easy to return to Michigan for a third NCAA season, but Werenski was ready to go pro. He signed a three-year entry-level contract with the Blue Jackets in March and reported to their AHL affiliate. Werenski dazzled with 14 points in 17 post-season games as the Lake Erie Monsters (now Cleveland Monsters) won the Calder Cup, sweeping the Hershey Bears in the finals.

Coming into training camp, Werenski was determined to impress taskmaster Jackets coach John Tortorella. The teen survived tough skating drills and approached his veteran teammates with a humble maturity. He made the opening-night roster and got an assist in a 6–3 loss to the Boston Bruins on October 13. It was a sign of things to come. Werenski averaged more than 20

minutes a night, often partnering with another young American star, Seth Jones. He also ran the top power-play unit, featuring captain Nick Foligno and leading scorer Cam Atkinson as the Jackets chased their first playoff berth since 2014.

Werenski's unselfish puck-moving style paid dividends. He shattered Ryan Murray's record for most points by a rookie Columbus defenceman (21) before the new year. The Jackets surprised the NHL when they forged a remarkable 16-game winning streak, the second longest in league history after the 1992–93 Pittsburgh Penguins (17). Columbus finished with a team-record 108 points, and Werenski had 11 goals and 36 assists in 78 games to top Rick Nash's old franchise rookie points mark (39).

Unfortunately, Werenski's dream season came to a rough end in the first round of the play-offs. In Game 3 versus the defending champion Pittsburgh Penguins, Columbus needed a win, trailing the series 2–0. Early in the first period, Werenski gave the Jackets a 3–1 lead with his first playoff goal on the power play. But midway through the game, a Phil Kessel shot hit him under the right eye, leaving a horrific cut. Werenski soldiered on, playing in the third period, but couldn't see well enough to play in overtime as Pittsburgh rallied to win, 5–4. That was the end of the playoffs for the 19-year-old, and the Penguins eliminated Columbus in five games.

Still, Werenski deservedly joined Auston Matthews and Patrik Laine as a 2017 Calder Trophy nominee for rookie of the year. He's still seven Norris Trophies behind Lidstrom, but one can expect this young man to collect some hardware during what looks to be a bright NHL career.

That Mats Zuccarello is a star in the NHL defies odds on two fronts. For starters, he is small. And second, he comes from Norway, not exactly a traditional pipeline to the NHL.

In 2004, teenaged Zuccarello started playing for Frisk in the Norwegian league, but he showed greater promise than that league's calibre could offer. But players just don't go from Norway to the NHL, and Zuccarello couldn't have imagined that as a career choice at that point. At 21, he signed with Modo for the 2008–09 season in Sweden's top league.

In his second season with Modo, he was named the league's MVP. All through his pro career, he also played for Norway internationally. This meant the full range of tournaments: the U18 (2004), U20 (2006), and World Championship (2008, 2009, 2010). He started to gain a wider audience at the 2010 Olympics in Vancouver, and that performance, combined with his MVP honour in Sweden, prompted the New York Rangers to sign him in the summer of 2010.

But his fight wasn't over by any stretch. Zuccarello was assigned to the AHL's Connecticut Whale to prove himself at yet another level up, and over two seasons he averaged nearly a point per game and had two lengthy stints with the Blueshirts. The lockout in 2012–13 didn't help, and he ended up in the KHL for the first half of the season before joining the Rangers down the stretch.

It wasn't really until September 2013 that he was a bona fide, full-time member of the Rangers, and he has been so ever since. Of course, he was never going to be a heavy hitter or even a player who could take control of a game on his own, but he was a very skilled forward who knew how to put the puck in the net.

In his first full season at age 26, he had 19 goals and 59 points, and the team made a surprise run to the Stanley Cup finals before losing to Los Angeles in five games.

## MATS ZUCCARELLO

B. OSLO, NORWAY, SEPTEMBER 1, 1987
5'7" 179 LBS.
RIGHT WING/SHOOTS LEFT
UNDRAFTED
NHL DEBUT DECEMBER 23, 2010
@ZUCCARELLO36

In his four full seasons since, he has been consistent at that pace, going on to record seasons of 49, 61, and 59 points through 2016–17. The Rangers have made the playoffs every year he has been with the team, so his participation in international events has been reduced to two major tournaments since the Vancouver Olympics: the 2014 Olympics and, as a member of Team Europe, the 2016 World Cup.

Zuccarello is an inspiration and an anomaly. A small player cut from the same determined cloth as Theo Fleury, Martin St. Louis, and Johnny Gaudreau, he is a rare Norwegian to make the NHL and one who seems to have many more miles left in the tank.

# APPENDIX

## CAREER STATISTICS

| | YEARS | REGULAR SEASON | | | | | PLAYOFFS | | | | |
|---|---|---|---|---|---|---|---|---|---|---|---|
| | | GP | G | A | P | PIM | GP | G | A | P | PIM |
| CAM ATKINSON | 2011–2017 | 382 | 121 | 106 | 227 | 102 | 11 | 3 | 3 | 6 | 0 |
| NICKLAS BACKSTROM | 2007–2017 | 734 | 188 | 540 | 728 | 372 | 96 | 26 | 49 | 75 | 48 |
| SVEN BAERTSCHI | 2011–2017 | 206 | 43 | 50 | 93 | 48 | 2 | 0 | 0 | 0 | 0 |
| ALEKSANDER BARKOV | 2013–2017 | 252 | 73 | 98 | 171 | 44 | 6 | 2 | 1 | 3 | 2 |
| JAMIE BENN | 2009–2017 | 585 | 218 | 299 | 517 | 450 | 19 | 9 | 11 | 20 | 14 |
| SAM BENNETT | 2014–2017 | 159 | 31 | 32 | 63 | 112 | 15 | 5 | 1 | 6 | 12 |
| ANDRE BURAKOVSKY | 2014–2017 | 196 | 38 | 57 | 95 | 36 | 36 | 6 | 4 | 10 | 8 |
| BRENT BURNS | 2003–2017 | 879 | 170 | 329 | 499 | 571 | 64 | 12 | 27 | 39 | 73 |
| SIDNEY CROSBY | 2005–2017 | 782 | 382 | 645 | 1,027 | 576 | 148 | 57 | 107 | 164 | 71 |
| MAX DOMI | 2015–2017 | 140 | 27 | 63 | 90 | 112 | -- | -- | -- | -- | -- |
| DREW DOUGHTY | 2008–2017 | 688 | 92 | 270 | 362 | 501 | 81 | 16 | 35 | 51 | 66 |
| LEON DRAISAITL | 2014–2017 | 191 | 50 | 87 | 137 | 44 | 13 | 6 | 10 | 16 | 19 |
| JONATHAN DROUIN | 2014–2017 | 164 | 29 | 66 | 95 | 54 | 23 | 5 | 9 | 14 | 16 |
| MATT DUCHENE | 2009–2017 | 572 | 174 | 244 | 418 | 140 | 8 | 0 | 6 | 6 | 2 |
| JORDAN EBERLE | 2010–2017 | 507 | 165 | 217 | 382 | 120 | 13 | 0 | 2 | 2 | 2 |
| NIKOLAJ EHLERS | 2015–2017 | 154 | 40 | 62 | 102 | 59 | -- | -- | -- | -- | -- |

| | | REGULAR SEASON | | | | | PLAYOFFS | | | | |
|---|---|---|---|---|---|---|---|---|---|---|---|
| | YEARS | GP | G | A | P | PIM | GP | G | A | P | PIM |
| JACK EICHEL | 2015–2017 | 142 | 48 | 65 | 113 | 44 | -- | -- | -- | -- | -- |
| AARON EKBLAD | 2014–2017 | 227 | 37 | 59 | 96 | 131 | 6 | 0 | 1 | 1 | 0 |
| FILIP FORSBERG | 2012–2017 | 264 | 91 | 100 | 191 | 107 | 42 | 15 | 11 | 26 | 20 |
| ALEX GALCHENYUK | 2012–2017 | 336 | 89 | 115 | 204 | 129 | 28 | 4 | 9 | 13 | 16 |
| JOHNNY GAUDREAU | 2013–2017 | 232 | 73 | 131 | 204 | 38 | 15 | 4 | 7 | 11 | 6 |
| SHAYNE GOSTISBEHERE | 2014–2017 | 142 | 24 | 61 | 85 | 56 | 6 | 1 | 1 | 2 | 4 |
| MIKAEL GRANLUND | 2012–2017 | 321 | 57 | 144 | 201 | 80 | 34 | 7 | 11 | 18 | 4 |
| TAYLOR HALL | 2010–2017 | 453 | 152 | 229 | 381 | 266 | -- | -- | -- | -- | -- |
| NOAH HANIFIN | 2015–2017 | 160 | 8 | 43 | 51 | 48 | -- | -- | -- | -- | -- |
| VICTOR HEDMAN | 2009–2017 | 549 | 65 | 236 | 301 | 431 | 65 | 6 | 31 | 37 | 30 |
| BO HORVAT | 2014–2017 | 231 | 49 | 68 | 117 | 61 | 6 | 1 | 3 | 4 | 2 |
| JONATHAN HUBERDEAU | 2012–2017 | 303 | 68 | 130 | 198 | 149 | 6 | 1 | 2 | 3 | 10 |
| PATRICK KANE | 2007–2017 | 740 | 285 | 467 | 752 | 284 | 127 | 50 | 73 | 123 | 62 |
| ERIK KARLSSON | 2009–2017 | 556 | 117 | 339 | 456 | 280 | 48 | 6 | 31 | 37 | 26 |
| ANZE KOPITAR | 2006–2017 | 840 | 255 | 481 | 736 | 228 | 75 | 20 | 44 | 64 | 39 |
| NIKITA KUCHEROV | 2013–2017 | 285 | 108 | 126 | 234 | 119 | 45 | 22 | 20 | 42 | 22 |
| PATRIK LAINE | 2016–2017 | 73 | 36 | 28 | 64 | 26 | -- | -- | -- | -- | -- |
| NATHAN MACKINNON | 2013–2017 | 300 | 75 | 131 | 206 | 96 | 7 | 2 | 8 | 10 | 4 |
| EVGENI MALKIN | 2006–2017 | 706 | 328 | 504 | 832 | 726 | 149 | 58 | 99 | 157 | 200 |
| MITCH MARNER | 2016–2017 | 77 | 19 | 42 | 61 | 38 | 6 | 1 | 3 | 4 | 0 |
| AUSTON MATTHEWS | 2016–2017 | 82 | 40 | 29 | 69 | 14 | 6 | 4 | 1 | 5 | 0 |
| CONNOR MCDAVID | 2015–2017 | 127 | 46 | 102 | 148 | 44 | 13 | 5 | 4 | 9 | 2 |
| SEAN MONAHAN | 2013–2017 | 319 | 107 | 110 | 217 | 58 | 15 | 7 | 4 | 11 | 2 |
| WILLIAM NYLANDER | 2015–2017 | 103 | 28 | 46 | 74 | 36 | 6 | 1 | 3 | 4 | 2 |
| ALEXANDER OVECHKIN | 2005–2017 | 921 | 558 | 477 | 1,035 | 617 | 97 | 46 | 44 | 90 | 46 |
| MAX PACIORETTY | 2008–2017 | 562 | 209 | 202 | 411 | 309 | 38 | 10 | 9 | 19 | 35 |
| ARTEMI PANARIN | 2015–2017 | 162 | 61 | 90 | 151 | 53 | 11 | 2 | 6 | 8 | 14 |
| DAVID PASTRNAK | 2014–2017 | 172 | 59 | 64 | 123 | 62 | 6 | 2 | 2 | 4 | 6 |
| SAM REINHART | 2014–2017 | 167 | 40 | 50 | 90 | 18 | -- | -- | -- | -- | -- |
| MORGAN RIELLY | 2013–2017 | 312 | 25 | 94 | 119 | 75 | 6 | 1 | 4 | 5 | 2 |
| RASMUS RISTOLAINEN | 2013–2017 | 273 | 25 | 85 | 110 | 123 | -- | -- | -- | -- | -- |
| MARK SCHEIFELE | 2011–2017 | 306 | 90 | 137 | 227 | 124 | 4 | 0 | 1 | 1 | 4 |
| TYLER SEGUIN | 2010–2017 | 508 | 189 | 238 | 427 | 140 | 49 | 7 | 14 | 21 | 6 |
| KEVIN SHATTENKIRK | 2010–2017 | 490 | 68 | 230 | 298 | 304 | 60 | 5 | 29 | 34 | 41 |
| STEVEN STAMKOS | 2008–2017 | 586 | 321 | 261 | 582 | 368 | 49 | 15 | 20 | 35 | 32 |
| MARK STONE | 2012–2017 | 249 | 75 | 112 | 187 | 83 | 27 | 5 | 8 | 13 | 22 |
| RYAN STROME | 2013–2017 | 258 | 45 | 81 | 126 | 123 | 15 | 3 | 5 | 8 | 4 |

| | | REGULAR SEASON | | | | | PLAYOFFS | | | | |
|---|---|---|---|---|---|---|---|---|---|---|---|
| | YEARS | GP | G | A | P | PIM | GP | G | A | P | PIM |
| P.K. SUBBAN | 2009–2017 | 500 | 73 | 245 | 318 | 576 | 77 | 13 | 37 | 50 | 123 |
| VLADAMIR TARASENKO | 2012–2017 | 341 | 145 | 139 | 284 | 106 | 44 | 22 | 10 | 32 | 2 |
| JOHN TAVARES | 2009–2017 | 587 | 235 | 302 | 537 | 281 | 24 | 11 | 11 | 22 | 12 |
| JONATHAN TOEWS | 2007–2017 | 717 | 272 | 350 | 622 | 390 | 128 | 40 | 70 | 110 | 82 |
| VINCENT TROCHECK | 2013–2017 | 228 | 60 | 77 | 137 | 117 | 2 | 0 | 1 | 1 | 0 |
| JAKE TROUBA | 2013–2017 | 271 | 31 | 74 | 105 | 205 | 4 | 0 | 2 | 2 | 2 |
| SHEA WEBER | 2005–2017 | 841 | 183 | 302 | 485 | 606 | 65 | 14 | 17 | 31 | 62 |
| ALEXANDER WENNBERG | 2014–2017 | 217 | 25 | 94 | 119 | 45 | 5 | 0 | 1 | 1 | 2 |
| ZACH WERENSKI | 2016–2017 | 78 | 11 | 36 | 47 | 14 | 3 | 1 | 0 | 1 | 0 |
| MATS ZUCCARELLO | 2010–2017 | 383 | 86 | 176 | 262 | 155 | 60 | 11 | 20 | 31 | 46 |

## TROPHIES

| | STANLEY CUP | CONN SMYTHE | ART ROSS | HART | ROCKET RICHARD | PEARSON/ LINDSAY | NORRIS | CALDER |
|---|---|---|---|---|---|---|---|---|
| JAMIE BENN | | | DAL 2015 | | | | | |
| BRENT BURNS | | | | | | | SJ 2017 | |
| SIDNEY CROSBY | PIT 2009, 2016, 2017 | PIT 2016, 2017 | PIT 2007, 2014 | PIT 2007, 2014 | PIT 2010 (share), 2017 | PIT 2007, 2013, 2014 | | |
| DREW DOUGHTY | LA 2012, 2014 | | | | | | | |
| AARON EKBLAD | | | | | | | | FLO 2015 |
| JONATHAN HUBERDEAU | | | | | | | | FLO 2013 |
| PATRICK KANE | CHI 2010, 2013, 2015 | CHI 2013 | | | | | | CHI 2008 |
| ERIK KARLSSON | | | | | | | OTT 2012, 2015 | |
| ANZE KOPITAR | LA 2012, 2014 | | | | | | | |
| NATHAN MACKINNON | | | | | | | | COL 2014 |
| EVGENI MALKIN | PIT 2009, 2016, 2017 | PIT 2009 | PIT 2009, 2012 | | | PIT 2012 | | PIT 2007 |
| AUSTON MATTHEWS | | | | | | | | TML 2017 |
| CONNOR MCDAVID | | | EDM 2017 | EDM 2017 | | EDM 2017 | | |

| | STANLEY CUP | CONN SMYTHE | ART ROSS | HART | ROCKET RICHARD | PEARSON/ LINDSAY | NORRIS | CALDER |
|---|---|---|---|---|---|---|---|---|
| ALEXANDER OVECHKIN | | | WAS 2008 | WAS 2008, 2009, 2013 | WAS 2008, 2009, 2013, 2014, 2015 | WAS 2008, 2009, 2010 | | WAS 2006 |
| STEVEN STAMKOS | | | | | TB 2010 (share), 2012 | | | |
| P.K. SUBBAN | | | | | | | MTL 2013 | |
| JONATHAN TOEWS | CHI 2010, 2013, 2015 | CHI 2010 | | | | | | |

# INTERNATIONAL STATISTICS

| | NAT | OLYMPICS | WORLD CHAMPIONSHIP | WORLD JUNIORS | WORLD U18 | WORLD CUP |
|---|---|---|---|---|---|---|
| CAM ATKINSON | USA | | 7th 2012 | | | |
| NICKLAS BACKSTROM | SWE | 5th 2010, silver 2014 | gold 2006, 4th 2007, 4th 2008, 6th 2012, gold 2017 | 5th 2006, 4th 2007 | bronze 2005 | 3rd 2016 |
| SVEN BAERTSCHI | SUI | | 10th 2014 | 5th 2011, 8th 2012 | 8th 2009, 5th 2010 | |
| ALEKSANDER BARKOV | FIN | bronze 2014 | 6th 2015, silver 2016 | 4th 2012, 7th 2013 | 4th 2012 | 8th 2016 |
| JAMIE BENN | CAN | gold 2014 | 5th 2012 | gold 2009 | | |
| SAM BENNETT | CAN | | | | gold 2013 | |
| ANDRE BURAKOVSKY | SWE | | 6th 2016 | silver 2014 | silver 2012, 5th 2013 | |
| BRENT BURNS | CAN | | silver 2008, 7th 2010, 5th 2011, gold 2015 | silver 2004 | | 1st 2016 |
| SIDNEY CROSBY | CAN | gold 2010, gold 2014 | 4th 2006, gold 2015 | silver 2004, gold 2005 | | 1st 2016 |
| MAX DOMI | CAN | | gold 2016 | gold 2015 | | |
| DREW DOUGHTY | CAN | gold 2010, gold 2014 | silver 2009 | gold 2008 | 4th 2007 | 1st 2016 |
| LEON DRAISAITL | GER | | 14th 2014, 7th 2016, 8th 2017 | 9th 2013, 9th 2014 | 6th 2012, 8th 2013 | 2nd 2016 (Europe) |
| JONATHAN DROUIN | CAN | | | 4th 2013, 4th 2014 | | 5th 2016 (North America) |

| | NAT | OLYMPICS | WORLD CHAMPIONSHIP | WORLD JUNIORS | WORLD U18 | WORLD CUP |
|---|---|---|---|---|---|---|
| **MATT DUCHENE** | CAN | gold 2014 | 7th 2010, 5th 2011, 5th 2013, gold 2015, gold 2016, silver 2017 | | gold 2008 | 1st 2016 |
| **JORDAN EBERLE** | CAN | | 7th 2010, 5th 2011, 5th 2012, 5th 2013, gold 2015 | gold 2009, silver 2010 | gold 2008 | |
| **NIKOLAJ EHLERS** | DEN | | 8th 2016 | 8th 2015 | | |
| **JACK EICHEL** | USA | | bronze 2015, 5th 2017 | 5th 2014, 5th 2015 | silver 2013, gold 2014 | 5th 2016 (North America) |
| **AARON EKBLAD** | CAN | | gold 2015 | 4th 2014 | | 5th 2016 (North America) |
| **FILIP FORSBERG** | SWE | | 5th 2015 | gold 2012, silver 2013, silver 2014 | silver 2011, silver 2012 | 3rd 2016 |
| **ALEX GALCHENYUK** | USA | | bronze 2013 | gold 2013 | | |
| **JOHNNY GAUDREAU** | USA | | 6th 2014, 5th 2017 | gold 2013 | | 5th 2016 (North America) |
| **SHAYNE GOSTISBEHERE** | USA | | | gold 2013 | | 5th 2016 (North America) |
| **MIKAEL GRANLUND** | FIN | bronze 2014 | gold 2011, 4th 2012, 4th 2013, silver 2016 | 7th 2009, 5th 2010, 4th 2012 | bronze 2009, bronze 2010 | 8th 2016 |
| **TAYLOR HALL** | CAN | | 5th 2013, gold 2015, gold 2016 | silver 2010 | gold 2008 | |
| **NOAH HANIFIN** | USA | | 4th 2016, 5th 2017 | 5th 2015 | gold 2014 | |
| **VICTOR HEDMAN** | SWE | | bronze 2010, 6th 2012, gold 2017 | silver 2008, silver 2009 | bronze 2007, 4th 2008 | 3rd 2016 |
| **BO HORVAT** | CAN | | | 4th 2014 | | |
| **JONATHAN HUBERDEAU** | CAN | | 5th 2014 | bronze 2012, 4th 2013 | | |
| **PATRICK KANE** | USA | silver 2010, 4th 2014 | 6th 2008 | bronze 2007 | gold 2006 | 7th 2016 |
| **ERIK KARLSSON** | SWE | silver 2014 | bronze 2010, 6th 2012 | silver 2009 | 4th 2008 | 3rd 2016 |
| **ANZE KOPITAR** | SLO | 7th 2014 | 16th 2006, 15th 2008, 16th 2015 | | | 2nd 2016 (Europe) |
| **NIKITA KUCHEROV** | RUS | | bronze 2017 | silver 2012, bronze 2013 | bronze 2011 | 4th 2016 |
| **PATRIK LAINE** | FIN | | silver 2016 | gold 2016 | silver 2015 | 8th 2016 |

| | NAT | OLYMPICS | WORLD CHAMPIONSHIP | WORLD JUNIORS | WORLD U18 | WORLD CUP |
|---|---|---|---|---|---|---|
| **NATHAN MACKINNON** | CAN | | 5th 2014, gold 2015, silver 2017 | | 4th 2013 | 5th 2016 (North America) |
| **EVGENI MALKIN** | RUS | 4th 2006, 6th 2010, 5th 2014 | bronze 2005, 5th 2006, bronze 2007, silver 2010, gold 2012, gold 2014, silver 2015 | 5th 2004, silver 2005, silver 2006 | bronze 2003, gold 2004 | 4th 2016 |
| **MITCH MARNER** | CAN | | silver 2017 | 6th 2016 | | |
| **AUSTON MATTHEWS** | USA | | 4th 2016 | 5th 2015, bronze 2016 | gold 2014, gold 2015 | 5th 2016 (North America) |
| **CONNOR MCDAVID** | CAN | | gold 2016 | 4th 2014, gold 2015 | gold 2013 | 5th 2016 (North America) |
| **SEAN MONAHAN** | CAN | | 5th 2014 | | | |
| **WILLIAM NYLANDER** | SWE | | gold 2017 | 4th 2015, 4th 2016 | 5th 2013, 4th 2014 | |
| **ALEXANDER OVECHKIN** | RUS | 4th 2006, 6th 2010, 5th 2014 | 10th 2004, bronze 2005, 5th 2006, bronze 2007, gold 2008, silver 2010, 4th 2011, gold 2012, 6th 2013, gold 2014, silver 2015, bronze 2016 | gold 2003, 5th 2004, silver 2005 | silver 2002, bronze 2003 | 6th 2004, 4th 2016 |
| **MAX PACIORETTY** | USA | 4th 2014 | 7th 2012 | 4th 2008 | | 7th 2016 |
| **ARTEMI PANARIN** | RUS | | silver 2015, bronze 2016 | gold 2011 | | 4th 2016 |
| **DAVID PASTRNAK** | CZE | | 5th 2016, 7th 2017 | 6th 2014, 6th 2015, 5th 2016 | 7th 2013, silver 2014 | 6th 2016 |
| **SAM REINHART** | CAN | | gold 2016 | 4th 2014, gold 2015 | bronze 2012, gold 2013 | |
| **MORGAN RIELLY** | CAN | | 5th 2014, gold 2016 | 4th 2013 | 4th 2011 | 5th 2016 (North America) |
| **RASMUS RISTOLAINEN** | FIN | | | 4th 2012, 7th 2013, gold 2014 | 4th 2012 | 8th 2016 |
| **MARK SCHEIFELE** | CAN | | 5th 2014, gold 2016, silver 2017 | bronze 2012, 4th 2013 | 4th 2011 | 5th 2016 (North America) |
| **TYLER SEGUIN** | CAN | | gold 2015 | | | |
| **KEVIN SHATTENKIRK** | USA | 4th 2014 | 8th 2011 | 5th 2009 | silver 2007 | |
| **STEVEN STAMKOS** | CAN | | silver 2009, 7th 2010, 5th 2013 | gold 2008 | 4th 2007 | 1st 2016 |
| **MARK STONE** | CAN | | gold 2016 | bronze 2012 | | |

| | NAT | OLYMPICS | WORLD CHAMPIONSHIP | WORLD JUNIORS | WORLD U18 | WORLD CUP |
|---|---|---|---|---|---|---|
| RYAN STROME | CAN | | | bronze 2012, 4th 2013 | | |
| P.K. SUBBAN | CAN | gold 2014 | 5th 2013 | gold 2008, gold 2009 | | |
| VLADAMIR TARASENKO | RUS | 5th 2014 | 4th 2011, silver 2015 | 6th 2010, gold 2011 | silver 2009 | 4th 2016 |
| JOHN TAVARES | CAN | gold 2014 | 7th 2010, 5th 2011, 5th 2012 | gold 2008, gold 2009 | 4th 2006 | 1st 2016 |
| JONATHAN TOEWS | CAN | gold 2010, gold 2014 | gold 2007, silver 2008 | gold 2006, gold 2007 | | 1st 2016 |
| VINCENT TROCHECK | USA | | 6th 2014 | gold 2013 | | 5th 2016 (North America) |
| JAKE TROUBA | USA | | bronze 2013, 6th 2014 | 7th 2012, gold 2013 | gold 2011, gold 2012 | 5th 2016 (North America) |
| SHEA WEBER | CAN | gold 2010, gold 2014 | gold 2007, silver 2009 | gold 2005 | | 1st 2016 |
| ALEXANDER WENNBERG | SWE | | 6th 2016 | silver 2013, silver 2014 | silver 2012 | |
| ZACH WERENSKI | USA | | | 5th 2015, bronze 2016 | | |
| MATS ZUCCARELLO | NOR | 10th 2010, 12th 2014 | 8th 2008, 11th 2009, 9th 2010, 10th 2016 | 10th 2006 | 10th 2004 | 2nd 2016 (Europe) |

# ALL-STAR TEAM SELECTIONS

| | POSITION | 1ST TEAM | 2ND TEAM |
|---|---|---|---|
| JAMIE BENN | left wing | 2013-14, 15-16 | 2014-15 |
| BRENT BURNS | defence | 2016-17 | 2015-16 |
| SIDNEY CROSBY | centre | 2006-07, 12-13, 13-14, 15-16 | 2009-10, 14-15, 16-17 |
| DREW DOUGHTY | defence | 2015-16 | 2009-10, 14-15 |
| VICTOR HEDMAN | defence | | 2016-17 |
| PATRICK KANE | right wing | 2009-10, 15-16, 16-17 | |
| ERIK KARLSSON | defence | 2011-12, 14-15, 15-16, 16-17 | |
| NIKITA KUCHEROV | right wing | | 2016-17 |
| EVGENI MALKIN | centre | 2007-08, 08-09, 11-12 | |
| CONNOR MCDAVID | centre | 2016-17 | |

| | POSITION | 1ST TEAM | 2ND TEAM |
|---|---|---|---|
| ALEXANDER OVECHKIN | left wing | 2005-06, 06-07, 07-08, 08-09, 09-10, 12-13*, 14-15 | 2010-11, 12-13*, 13-14**, 15-16 |
| ARTEMI PANARIN | left wing | | 2016-17 |
| STEVEN STAMKOS | centre | | 2010-11, 11-12 |
| P.K. SUBBAN | defence | 2012-13, 14-15 | |
| VLADAMIR TARASENKO | right wing | | 2014-15, 15-16 |
| JOHN TAVARES | centre | 2014-15 | |
| JONATHAN TOEWS | centre | | 2012-13 |
| SHEA WEBER | defence | 2010-11, 11-12 | 2013-14, 14-15 |

* erroneously named to both teams by NHL, 1st team as right wing, 2nd team as left wing

** right wing

# ALL-STAR GAME STATISTICS

| | YEAR | G | A | P | PIM |
|---|---|---|---|---|---|
| CAM ATKINSON | 2017 | 3 | 2 | 5 | 0 |
| NICKLAS BACKSTROM | 2016 | 0 | 0 | 0 | 0 |
| JAMIE BENN | 2012 | 0 | 0 | 0 | 0 |
| | 2016 | 0 | 1 | 1 | 0 |
| BRENT BURNS | 2011 | 0 | 1 | 1 | 0 |
| | 2015 | 1 | 1 | 2 | 0 |
| | 2016 | 0 | 4 | 4 | 0 |
| | 2017 | 1 | 1 | 2 | 0 |
| SIDNEY CROSBY | 2007 | 0 | 0 | 0 | 0 |
| | 2017 | 1 | 1 | 2 | 0 |
| DREW DOUGHTY | 2015 | 0 | 1 | 1 | 0 |
| | 2016 | 1 | 1 | 2 | 0 |
| | 2017 | 1 | 3 | 4 | 0 |
| MATT DUCHENE | 2011 | 1 | 0 | 1 | 0 |
| | 2016 | 0 | 2 | 2 | 0 |
| JORDAN EBERLE | 2012 | 0 | 1 | 1 | 0 |
| AARON EKBLAD | 2015 | 0 | 4 | 4 | 0 |
| | 2016 | 1 | 0 | 1 | 0 |
| FILIP FORSBERG | 2015 | 2 | 0 | 2 | 0 |
| JOHNNY GAUDREAU | 2015 | 0 | 2 | 2 | 0 |
| | 2016 | 1 | 2 | 3 | 0 |
| | 2017 | 2 | 2 | 4 | 0 |

| | YEAR | G | A | P | PIM |
|---|---|---|---|---|---|
| TAYLOR HALL | 2016 | 2 | 1 | 3 | 0 |
| | 2017 | 1 | 3 | 4 | 0 |
| VICTOR HEDMAN | 2017 | 0 | 1 | 1 | 0 |
| BO HORVAT | 2017 | 2 | 2 | 4 | 0 |
| PATRICK KANE | 2009 | 1 | 1 | 2 | 0 |
| | 2011 | 0 | 1 | 1 | 0 |
| | 2012 | 1 | 0 | 1 | 0 |
| | 2015 | 2 | 1 | 3 | 0 |
| | 2016 | 1 | 0 | 1 | 0 |
| | 2017 | 0 | 0 | 0 | 0 |
| ERIK KARLSSON | 2011 | 0 | 0 | 0 | 0 |
| | 2012 | 0 | 0 | 0 | 0 |
| | 2016 | 1 | 0 | 1 | 0 |
| | 2017 | 1 | 0 | 1 | 0 |
| ANZE KOPITAR | 2008 | 0 | 0 | 0 | 0 |
| | 2011 | 2 | 0 | 2 | 0 |
| | 2015 | 0 | 0 | 0 | 0 |
| NIKITA KUCHEROV | 2017 | 2 | 1 | 3 | 0 |
| PATRIK LAINE | 2017 | 0 | 0 | 0 | 0 |
| NATHAN MACKINNON | 2017 | 0 | 0 | 0 | 0 |
| EVGENI MALKIN | 2008 | 0 | 2 | 2 | 0 |
| | 2009 | 1 | 0 | 1 | 0 |

| | YEAR | G | A | P | PIM | | YEAR | G | A | P | PIM |
|---|---|---|---|---|---|---|---|---|---|---|---|
| EVGENI MALKIN cont'd | 2012 | 1 | 1 | 2 | 0 | VLADAMIR TARASENKO | 2015 | 0 | 4 | 4 | 0 |
| | 2016 | 1 | 1 | 2 | 0 | | 2016 | 0 | 2 | 2 | 0 |
| AUSTON MATTHEWS | 2017 | 1 | 0 | 1 | 0 | | 2017 | 1 | 0 | 1 | 0 |
| CONNOR MCDAVID | 2017 | 2 | 2 | 4 | 0 | JOHN TAVARES | 2012 | 1 | 1 | 2 | 0 |
| ALEXANDER OVECHKIN | 2007 | 1 | 0 | 1 | 0 | | 2015 | 4 | 0 | 4 | 0 |
| | 2008 | 2 | 0 | 2 | 0 | | 2016 | 0 | 0 | 0 | 0 |
| | 2009 | 1 | 2 | 3 | 0 | | 2017 | 2 | 3 | 5 | 0 |
| | 2011 | 1 | 1 | 2 | 0 | JONATHAN TOEWS | 2009 | 1 | 0 | 1 | 0 |
| | 2015 | 0 | 3 | 3 | 0 | | 2011 | 1 | 2 | 3 | 0 |
| | 2017 | 1 | 1 | 2 | 0 | | 2015 | 1 | 4 | 5 | 0 |
| TYLER SEGUIN | 2012 | 0 | 1 | 1 | 0 | | 2017 | 1 | 0 | 1 | 0 |
| | 2015 | 2 | 2 | 4 | 0 | VINCENT TROCHECK | 2017 | 1 | 2 | 3 | 0 |
| | 2016 | 1 | 2 | 3 | 0 | SHEA WEBER | 2009 | 0 | 0 | 0 | 0 |
| | 2017 | 0 | 2 | 2 | 0 | | 2011 | 0 | 4 | 4 | 0 |
| KEVIN SHATTENKIRK | 2015 | 1 | 1 | 2 | 0 | | 2012 | 0 | 0 | 0 | 0 |
| STEVEN STAMKOS | 2011 | 1 | 0 | 1 | 0 | | 2015 | 0 | 1 | 1 | 0 |
| | 2012 | 0 | 1 | 1 | 0 | | 2016 | 0 | 2 | 2 | 0 |
| | 2015 | 2 | 1 | 3 | 0 | | 2017 | 0 | 1 | 1 | 0 |
| | 2016 | 0 | 0 | 0 | 0 | | | | | | |
| P.K. SUBBAN | 2016 | 1 | 0 | 1 | 0 | | | | | | |
| | 2017 | 1 | 0 | 1 | 0 | | | | | | |

* no all-star game in 2002, 2006, 2010, 2014 (Olympics) or 2005, 2013 (lockout)

# ACKNOWLEDGEMENTS

I'd like to thank the many people at ECW Press for their energy and enthusiasm in making what is hopefully a worthy addition to their hockey-book library. Notably, publisher Jack David and his colleague Michael Holmes. As well to editor Laura Pastore and designer Troy Cunningham. Importantly, a special thanks to Rob Del Mundo, Carol Schram, and Lucas Aykroyd for help in putting these bios together. Their expert writing and research skills are second to none. To my family — Liz, Ian, Zac, Emily — and especially my mom, who bought me my first pair of skates (and second, and third). And lastly, to my wife, who supports my continued efforts to play pickup by doing something else whenever I'm skating.

# PHOTO CREDITS

Jonathan Drouin

    (41) REUTERS/Brendan McDermid - RTX117FQ

Matt Duchene

    (43) REUTERS/Joshua Lott - RTXXL7J

Jordan Eberle

    (45) REUTERS/Shaun Best - RTR232YR

Nikolaj Ehlers

    (49) Noah K. Murray/USA TODAY Sports - RTX31EHO

Jack Eichel

    (51) Tom Szczerbowski/USA TODAY Sports - RTS9QSY

Aaron Ekblad

    (55) Tom Szczerbowski/USA TODAY Sports - RTSAZS8

Filip Forsberg

    (57) Christopher Hanewinckel/USA TODAY Sports - RTS14KZQ

Alex Galchenyuk

    (59) Jean-Yves Ahern/USA TODAY Sports - RTX32GRR

Johnny Gaudreau

    (63) Sergei Belski/USA TODAY Sports - RTX2VERJ

Shayne Gostisbehere

    (67) Jean-Yves Ahern/USA TODAY Sports - RTX27S03

Mikael Granlund

    (69) Candice Ward/USA TODAY Sports - RTSUFG8

Taylor Hall

    (71) Ed Mulholland/USA TODAY Sports - RTSUZL1

Noah Hanifin

    (73) James Guillory/USA TODAY Sports - RTX1V4AD

Victor Hedman

    (75) Dan Hamilton/USA TODAY Sports - RTX2QGBM

Bo Horvat

    (77) David Banks/USA TODAY Sports - RTSWVSX

Jonathan Huberdeau

    (79) REUTERS/John Gress - RTX10PDC

Patrick Kane

    (81) Jasen Vinlove/USA TODAY Sports - RTX2BN2E

Erik Karlsson

    (85) Marc DesRosiers/USA TODAY Sports - RTX31EBZ

Anze Kopitar

    (89) REUTERS/Mike Blake - RTR33GP5

Nikita Kucherov

    (91) Brad Penner/USA TODAY Sports - RTX30VHD

Patrik Laine

    (93) Bruce Fedyck/USA TODAY Sports - RTX2WWP9

Nathan MacKinnon

    (97) Dan Hamilton/USA TODAY Sports - RTX2UKYZ

Evgeni Malkin

    (99) Charles LeClaire/USA TODAY Sports - RTSZ2CB

Mitch Marner

    (103) Dan Hamilton/USA TODAY Sports - RTX2X6OD

Auston Matthews

    (105) Tom Szczerbowski/USA TODAY Sports - RTX34H2I

Connor McDavid

    (109) Perry Nelson/USA TODAY Sports - RTX26L2J

Sean Monahan

    (113) Sergei Belski/USA TODAY Sports - RTX31KFO

William Nylander

    (115) John E. Sokolowski/USA TODAY Sports - RTSBKBF

Alexander Ovechkin

    (117) Geoff Burke/USA TODAY Sports - RTS149L9

Max Pacioretty

    (121) Adam Hunger/USA TODAY Sports - RTS10PIM

Artemi Panarin

    (123) Charles LeClaire/USA TODAY Sports - RTX33AIK

David Pastrnak

    (125) Bob DeChiara/USA TODAY Sports - RTSY7Q7s

Sam Reinhart

    (127) Dan Hamilton/USA TODAY Sports - RTSY85Z

Morgan Rielly

    (129) Tom Szczerbowski/USA TODAY Sports - RTS1037Q

Rasmus Ristolainen

    (131) Anne-Marie Sorvin/USA TODAY Sports - RTX2PSQX

Mark Scheifele

    (133) Tom Szczerbowski/USA TODAY Sports - RTR4QKLC

Tyler Seguin

    (137) REUTERS/Laszlo Balogh - RTX1DD7R

Kevin Shattenkirk

    (141) REUTERS/Sarah Conard - RTR2KD3U

Steven Stamkos

    (143) REUTERS/Steve Nesius - RTR2MWRE

Mark Stone

    (145) Charles LeClaire/USA TODAY Sports - RTSUTLK

Ryan Strome

    (147) Brad Penner/USA TODAY Sports - RTSU41L

P.K. Subban

    (149) Christopher Hanewinckel/USA TODAY Sports - RTS12PKJ

Vladamir Tarasenko

    (151) Jeff Curry/USA TODAY Sports - RTS14EYP

John Tavares

    (153) REUTERS/Shannon Stapleton - RTXZEB0

Jonathan Toews

    (155) Dennis Wierzbicki/USA TODAY Sports - RTX1GNNO

Vincent Trocheck

    (159) Steve Mitchell/USA TODAY Sports - RTX2XKSL

Jacob Trouba

    (161) Jayne Kamin-Oncea/USA TODAY Sports - RTSVKKB

Shea Weber

    (163) Tom Szczerbowski/USA TODAY Sports - RTSTH43

Alexander Wennberg

    (167) Aaron Doster/USA TODAY Sports - RTSS65D

Zach Werenski

    (169) Russell LaBounty/USA TODAY Sports - RTX2RZUL

Mats Zuccarello

    (171) Adam Hunger/USA TODAY Sports - RTX2WOAF